DUNKIRK

BATTLE STANDARDS MILITARY PAPERBACKS FROM DAVID & CHARLES

BATTLE STANDARDS

DUNKIRK

THE STORMS OF WAR

JOHN HARRIS

A DAVID & CHARLES MILITARY BOOK

British Library Cataloguing in Publication Data

Harris, John
  Dunkirk: the storms of war.
  1. Great Britain. *Army. British*
  Expeditionary Force
  2. Dunkirk, France, Battle of, 1940
  I. Title
  940.54'21   D756.5.D

  ISBN 0-7153-9202-6

First published 1980 in hardback by David & Charles Publishers plc
This paperback edition published 1988 by David & Charles
Publishers plc and printed in Great Britain
by Redwood Burn Limited, Trowbridge, Wiltshire
for David & Charles Publishers plc
Brunel House Newton Abbot Devon

Distributed in the US by Sterling Publishing Co. Inc.
2 Park Avenue, New York, NY 10016

Cover photographs
Front: Painting by C. Cundall of the evacuation from Dunkirk
        under air attack in June 1940. (Imperial War Museum,
        London; trans from MARS, Lincs)
Back: The streets of Dunkirk under German occupation,
        June 1940. (Colorific!)

CONTENTS

'I have myself full confidence that if all do their duty and nothing is neglected and if the best arrangements are made, we shall prove ourselves once again able to defend our island home, ride out the storms of war, and outlive the menace of tyranny if necessary for years, if necessary alone. At any rate, that is what we are trying to do. That is the resolve of the Government, every man of them. It is the will of Parliament and of the nation.

The British Empire with the French Republic, linked together in their cause and in their need, will defend to the death their native soil, aiding each other like good comrades to the utmost of their strength, even though large tracts of Europe and many old and famous States have fallen or may fall into the grip of the Gestapo and all the odious apparatus of Nazi rule.

We cannot flag or fail. We shall go on to the end. We shall fight in France, we shall fight on the seas and oceans, we shall fight with growing confidence and growing strength in the air. We shall defend our island whatever the cost may be. We shall fight on the beaches, we shall fight on the landing-grounds, in the fields, in the streets, and in the hills.

We shall never surrender, and even if, which I do not for a moment believe, this island or a large part of it were subjugated and starving, then our Empire beyond the seas, armed and guarded by the British Fleet, will carry on the struggle until in God's good time the New World, with all its power and might, sets forth to the liberation and rescue of the Old.'

Winston Churchill
House of Commons

4 June 1940

PREFACE

For the British people, 1940 was an incredible year. It was the one year of World War II which nobody who lived through it will ever forget. It was a year of history that began in the gloom and frustration of the black-out and the Phoney War, and ended with the British people having been through Dunkirk, the Battle of Britain and the Blitz.

From a smug self-satisfaction which, throughout the country from the Cabinet downwards, was reflected in the view that the British Empire could never be beaten, Britain descended to the brink of disaster, where she was to cling tooth and nail, alone and unaided, until the entry of Russia and then the United States into the war made certain its end. It was a traumatic year, and of everything that happened probably nothing created quite such a shock as the first great disaster, Dunkirk.

To the men then serving in the Forces, the word 'Dunkirk' is still tremendously evocative. In the way that names like Mons, the Somme and Passchendaele could be unbelievably moving to the men of World War I, so Dunkirk, Alamein and D-Day have become to those who grew to manhood after 1918. And, in the way that Mons sums up for that earlier generation the picture of a battered small army fighting with skill and courage against tremendous odds, so does Dunkirk to the later one.

Dunkirk produced a whole crop of legends, chief among which was that hundreds of amateur yachtsmen spontaneously leapt in a body to the rescue of the British Expeditionary Force with their weekend boats. It was not so. The evacuation of troops from Dunkirk was the result of foresight and planning and, despite the undoubted and splendid assistance of civilians, the largest percentage of the troops were rescued by Navy-manned vessels, while most of the civilians who took part were professional seamen—merchant sailors, fishermen, trawlermen and operators of harbour craft.

In addition to the seaborne operation, it should not be forgotten that Dunkirk was a military operation also—a hard-fought retreat with a magnificent last stand by the rearguard to allow the bulk of the troops to get clear. The actions of the three Services cannot be separated. The Navy could never have done what it did if the Army had not disengaged itself so successfully. The Royal Air Force's contribution, small as it had to be, was also vital.

This book does not attempt to tell the whole story of the retreat and evacuation, and does not cover the history of all the units involved. To attempt to describe the period in detail would merely be confusing to the reader, so, instead, I have tried to give a broad view, concentrating on the sound and the feel and the smell, which, after all, is as much the stuff of history as dates and figures. I have tried also to let events appear in chronological order and as near as possible to the time when they occurred, something that was not always easy, because Dunkirk happened a long time ago and as memories fade, dates grow confused. Nevertheless, I am very much indebted to the Dunkirk Veterans' Association and to those ex-soldiers, sailors and airmen, now growing old, who told me their stories with such surprising modesty.

THE FRONT CRUMBLES

Ever since 3 September 1939, first the French, then—as soon as they could take up their positions—the British, had faced the Germans along the Franco–German border.

The war had been a long time coming—ever since 1918, when French demands for reparations after World War I had beggared Germany, yet at the same time had prevented her earning the means to pay them. But while the 10 million dead of that war laid a cold shadow over the generation they had died to save, isolationism in America, pacifism in England and defeatism in France had been matched by increasingly aggressive demands by Germany to return to her full status, that made it easy for Adolf Hitler to stir up trouble.

Feeling they had been cheated in World War I, deprived of their colonies and the Saar, forced to give back Alsace-Lorraine, and with the Rhineland occupied and Danzig a free city, the Germans were ripe for Nazi theories. Marshal Foch, the Allied leader at the end of World War I, had realised that what had happened in 1918 was not peace, only a break in hostilities. His 'armistice for 20 years' was a remarkably accurate forecast. Bitterness and propaganda helped Hitler on his road to vengeance, aided all the way by woolly-minded dreamers at the League of Nations, whose good intentions for the most part seemed to consist of depriving their own country of arms while not depriving Germany.

Most people in Europe hated the thought of another conflict. They were terrified by the development of modern weapons, particularly bombers, and, trading on these fears, Hitler prepared for war and chose the moment for launching it. From the minute he came to power it was inevitable.

While weak statesmanship had permitted Germany to grow stronger and stronger, the war weariness that followed 1918, financial crises, the worst depression in living memory and a variety of pacifist movements had brought the British armed services to a dangerous level of inadequacy. As Clement Attlee acidly remarked, 'There seemed to be a feeling that an inefficient army was more moral than an efficient army'.

The Royal Navy had managed to retain most of its strength, though much of it was out of date. The RAF by acquiring sufficient single-wing Spitfires and Hurricanes to replace its obsolete biplanes during the breathing space afforded by Prime Minister Neville Chamberlain's concessions to Hitler at Munich, could match the German Luftwaffe in quality, though never in quantity. The Army, however, was in poor shape equipment-wise, though never in spirit. Only a few far-sighted officers had realised that the tank, that British World War I invention, was the symbol of the new type of warfare, with the result that in Britain when war began there was virtually no tank force worth noting—at a time when the Germans had evolved the Blitzkrieg.

The Germans were well aware of British weaknesses because German military attachés had seen infantrymen on manoeuvres in 1939 carrying placards to represent tanks or guns, a practice so widespread that, according to Lieutenant-General Sir Brian Horrocks, one young officer on receiving his first order to move into the North African desert asked if the enemy understood that a green flag represented a tank. Another officer, on a staff course, taken to task for placing an imaginary anti-tank gun up a tree, complained he had never seen an anti-tank gun and had no idea what they were like.

Yet the Germans had been allowed to repudiate the Versailles Treaty, made at the end of World War I, to snatch back land taken from them under that treaty, and, as they realised no one was willing to oppose them, to rearm, and finally to demand more and more. Austria and Czechoslovakia had been swept into the German net and Albania and Abyssinia into that of her ally, Italy. Only when Germany attacked Poland after a fabricated border incident were Britain and France finally shamed into going to war to help a country it was virtually impossible to get at, and Poland went down to defeat in a mere three weeks. Now, in 1940, with the German Siegfried Line and the French Maginot Line between them, it was equally difficult to get at the Germans and, since they seemed quiescent, a feeling began to grow in Britain that this war which nobody wanted, like the proverbial old soldier, was quietly going to fade away.

The Maginot Line, in fact, was nothing but an illusion. It had been built by André Maginot, whose experiences as a sergeant in World War I had shaped his thinking, and 2,900 million francs were spent on its fortifications. With its deep underground barrack rooms and guns that commanded every possible line of approach, it was tremendously strong. Unfortunately, it ended in mid-air: from

Longuyon, near the Belgian border, to the North Sea 200 miles away there was no defence at all.

Unfortunately, this very area, the Flanders plain, is the natural approach to France and had been used countless times by invading armies. So, aware that, with much of France's industry concentrated in a deep salient in the north, such a sweep west could result in the swift capture of much of her war potential, to guard against this the frontier was manned by five armies, the intention being, when the battle started, to carry it to the enemy by swinging forward into Belgium.

By the spring of 1940 it was the view of General Maurice Gamelin, the Supreme Commander of the Allied Forces, that a German attack in the Ardennes further south was not practicable and he organised his forces accordingly. Two plans had been prepared: Plan E, a limited advance to the River Escaut (called by the Belgians the Scheldt), and Plan D, an advance to the River Dyle to cover Brussels and Antwerp. Since the French Seventh and First Armies and the British Expeditionary Force (BEF) were mechanised, they were chosen to carry out Plan D, but, unhappily, at the crucial point of the wheel were the French Ninth and Second Armies, two of the weakest in the French line.

It had been a bitter winter, with most of the casualties coming from black-outs and fouls in football matches. To the British, the French seemed to show a marked indifference to the war. According to Sir Basil Bartlett, then a young Intelligence captain, almost every house in the Rue Edouard Anseele in Roubaix was a brothel and he considered that the inhabitants would as happily sell France as themselves. In fact, most of the French were patriotic enough but after years of uncertain ruling by the same old gang, they were curiously apathetic and the propaganda poster most often seen was one which said, 'Nous vaincrons parce que nous sommes les plus forts', We shall conquer because we are the stronger, which to Bartlett seemed a curiously uninspired way of putting the point across.

The French staff were impressive. According to Bartlett, they wore what medals they liked—none if they were depressed, everything they could find if in good spirits—'pinned haphazardly on their tunics, like patterns for new curtains'. On one occasion he watched officers of a French mission pluck flowers and, not knowing what to do with them, hand them to a red-faced and furious British colonel who was obliged to carry them around until they left. Everybody accepted that the Germans were going to be difficult to beat and little had happened so far to encourage the morale of the Allies. Among the

French there was a definite feeling that the German soldier was a superman. Though they continued to say 'Ils ne passeront pas', They shall not pass, they had grown less and less convinced of the fact.

The British were surprisingly different. According to the French, their vehicles were excellent and there was a good relationship between officers and men.Everybody was enthusiastic and, with the promise of spring after a winter spent doing a great deal of digging and not much shooting, they were full of life. Their chief weakness was in tanks. Thanks to Treasury tight-fistedness, few had been built and, according to Bob Crisp, the South African test cricketer who was to win a DSO and an MC fighting with them, the design had been conceived by a pressure group obsessed with the obsolete idea that a tank should be as much like a horse as possible. 'The Charge of the Light Brigade,' Crisp said, 'was their idea of the proper way to fight a battle', and the fast lightly-armed tank was the result.

The animosity between the French and the British built up. To the French the British did not seem very professional and, as the propaganda from Radio Stuttgart hastened to point out, while most French soldiers were along the Franco–German frontier, behind the lines people were in the habit of pointing out to the British for a small *pourboire* the homes of those women whose husbands were away.

As spring arrived, everybody in France grew more and more certain that an attack was coming, and James Langley, a twenty-three-year-old subaltern in the 2nd Coldstream Guards near Lille, found himself practising retreat and rearguard exercises. His company commander's doctrine was simple: 'We always start a war with a retreat . . . What makes you think it will be different this time?'

In England, the Government, which had singularly failed to utilise the empty period of the Phoney War to produce any national martial ardour, was more inclined to the view that the war would end without fighting. 'Hitler,' the Prime Minister said on 4 April, 'has missed the bus.'

It was characteristic of the unhappy men who were running Britain, 'peace-loving men trying to steel themselves to bloody resolution', and characteristic of Hitler, too, that four days later German forces attacked Denmark and Norway. Although Britain had been expecting an attack in the north for some time—indeed, Winston Churchill, at the Admiralty, had even seemed to be trying to provoke one—the country was caught without the means to help the Norwegians. For the most part the troops that were sent were inexperienced and lacking in transport, weapons and air support, and the Norwegians were disgusted, claiming that they went into the line with four footballs and 50,000 cigarettes to a battalion and little else. By the end of the month they were struggling to salvage something from what was an obvious defeat.

The Norwegian campaign, however, was far from being an unmitigated disaster because German naval losses were very heavy—an advantage that was not as apparent at the time as it was to be a few weeks later. It also had the effect of removing Neville Chamberlain from the premiership and replacing him with the virile Churchill, who was to prove the voice and spirit of beleaguered Britain. On Tuesday 7 May, with the Government and particularly Churchill under fire in the House of Commons, Leopold Amery, not normally the most inspiring of speakers, rose to deflect the attack away from Churchill to Chamberlain and the general conduct of the war. He ended by quoting Cromwell's words to the Long Parliament: 'You have sat too long here for any good you are doing. Depart, I say, and let us have done with you. In the name of God, go!' By 10 May, Churchill was Prime Minister. And just in time, because in the early hours of that day he was awakened by the ringing of his bedside telephone. The Germans had struck again.

Despite all the blandishments of the British and the French, Belgium and Holland had resisted every effort to allow their borders with Germany to be fortified. They had watched Czechoslovakia, Austria, Poland, and now Denmark and Norway go down, unaided by the Allies, and terrified of their powerful neighbour to the east, they wanted only to keep their neutrality. They were on the horns of a terrible dilemma. They could not trust the Germans, yet, despite the fact that they needed the Allies' help, they did not dare show favour towards them in case the Germans found in it an excuse to invade.

Since the Maginot Line ended at the junction of the French and Belgian borders, the British had spent the winter continuing it with tank traps and pillboxes. Thousands of tons of concrete and miles of barbed wire were set down. How they would have withstood a panzer attack cannot be told because they were never called on to do so. When, at first light on 10 May, the German tanks rolled forward on a front extending from the North Sea to the Swiss frontier, Gamelin immediately put into operation the Allied counterplan for the advance into Belgium and, leaving their fortifications behind them, nine British divisions advanced in line with the French armies on either flank. 'I could have wept for joy,' Hitler said. They had fallen into the trap.'

During the night of 9–10 May there were air raids, anti-aircraft firing and searchlights. For No 1 Squadron, RAF, flying Hurricanes, it had been a normal day and Flying Officer Paul Richey had spent his spare time in Metz, watching the parade of French officers and *troupes de forteresse* from the Maginot Line with their black berets and badges inscribed with 'On ne passe pas'. Then, as the evening shadows lengthened and the sun touched the turrets and spires of the city, he noticed a faint sound, growing more distinct until it became a heavy rumbling like thunder. It was guns, he realised, and big ones, too. At 3.30 next morning, he was awakened after only two hours sleep. There were aircraft plots all over the board and by 5 am two flights were airborne, looking for German planes.

James Langley's awakening was more leisurely and typical of the Guards. His Guardsman servant arrived with a bright 'Good morning, sir. Here's your tea. Your bath's ready. It's a fine morning. The Germans invaded France, Belgium and Holland at dawn.'

Indeed they had, and a message had been received by General Lord Gort, commanding the BEF, to put Plan D into effect. At 1 pm the first vehicle of the 12th Royal Lancers, under Lieutenant-Colonel Herbert Lumsden, crossed into Belgium.

John Standish Surtees Prendergast Vereker, 6th Viscount Gort, was essentially a fighting soldier. A square, burly man, he had won the VC, three DSOs and the MC with the Grenadier Guards in World War I. Known as 'Tiger' to the press (though never to the troops who preferred to call him 'Fat Boy'), he held a very difficult position. Although to the British he appeared to be on equal footing with Gamelin, in fact, between them in the chain of command were two other officers, General Billotte, the Army Group Commander, and General Georges, the Commander North-East Front; and, while he was responsible to Britain for the safety of the BEF, to the French he was nothing more than an army commander among other army commanders.

Fifty-three years old and a man who enjoyed the excitement of war, Gort was not popular because he had been advanced out of his turn over the heads of senior officers by Leslie Hore-Belisha, War Minister until the beginning of 1940. He was a simple man who preferred a spartan kind of living and it had been said about him in his youth that he slept on a bed of concrete sluiced down every day with a bucket of cold water. There was also a popular saying, 'Oh, Gort, our help in ages past', which was usually uttered with more than just a touch of bitter sarcasm.

Certainly he was not a great strategist or a deep thinker and he could not stand up at a conference and deliver a clear military appreciation, yet, where a more brilliant soldier might have lost his nerve in the approaching crisis, Gort showed the one essential quality required at times of stress—mental toughness. It was thanks to his sound judgement that the BEF was saved from destruction.

The combined French, British, Belgian and Dutch armies had a numerical superiority over the Germans and almost twice as many tanks. These were mostly French and mostly better armoured, though less mobile, but they had been split up into penny packets for infantry support, so that when the great attacks came there were never enough of the Germans to halt them. Only in the air did the Germans hold a clear advantage. The French began the campaign with fewer than 100 bombers, of which only 25 were modern, and there were 256 light bombers—mostly obsolescent Battles and Blenheims—of the British Advanced Air Striking Force under Air Marshal Sir Arthur Barratt.

That particular morning, Sir Brian Horrocks, to become one of the war's best fighting generals but at that time only a brevet lieutenant-colonel at the Staff College, Camberley, was awakened like James Langley with the news that the war had come to life. He had already been informed that he was to take command of the 2nd Middlesex in France and the news prompted him to leave at once. Borrowing £2 from his ATS driver, he arrived in France the same day and, having studied Plan D and knowing the routes, he waited by the roadside for a lift. He became, he claimed, the first commander ever to enter battle in a dental truck. He had been to war twice before, in 1914, as a boy barely out of school, and again in 1919, in the Russian Civil War. Both times he had been taken prisoner.

By 10.30 that night the 12th Lancers had reached the line of the Dyle unopposed. The advance had been a complete success and at only one point, on the front of Major-General Bernard Law Montgomery, of the 3rd Division, was there any difficulty: the British were refused entry into Belgium on the grounds that they did not have the necessary permits, but a 15 cwt truck charged the barrier and the advance continued.

There was practically no interference from the Luftwaffe, and the French Seventh Army on the left of the BEF drove across Flanders to the estuary of the Scheldt and beyond it into Holland. On the right, the French First Army, under General Blanchard, moved to its assigned position between the Dyle and the Meuse. Unfortunately, General Corap's Ninth Army, at the hinge of the wheel, lacking transport and possessing virtually no regular officers, failed to stick to its timetable—with disastrous results.

Originally, the German plan, Fall Gelb—Plan Yellow—was in effect the same one that had been used in 1914. Thirty-seven divisions, eight armoured and two motorised, were to smash across Holland and the Belgian plain and break through the Franco–Belgian frontier in the level country of Flanders. A secondary attack was to be made through Luxembourg, chiefly to pin down French reserves and threaten the Maginot Line. But, about the time General Gamelin was coming to the conclusion that the Ardennes was impossible country for a major armoured assault, the Germans had abandoned their first version of Plan Yellow and the emphasis of the attack was moved south. Full opportunities were given to armour and speed, while Army Group B, advancing in the north, was cut down to twenty-eight divisions.

As General Corap's Ninth Army, with its horse-drawn transport and squadrons of horsed cavalry, moved up, forty-four German divisions, seven armoured and three motorised, thundered through the Ardennes, General Ewald Von Kleist's panzer group in the van. The thin Belgian resistance was overwhelmed and the cavalry of the French Ninth Army brushed aside, and within three days Major General Erwin Rommel, with the 7th Panzer Division, was crossing the Meuse near Sedan. That same day, two other crossings were made and Corap's army was shattered.

It was as the first shots were fired by the British that Horrocks took over the 2nd Middlesex at Louvain. He was under Montgomery, something he did not look forward to: Montgomery was not a popular figure, and he did not expect to last very long. Immediately he had his first lesson in practical command. The Ulster Rifles had been very heavily shelled; the Germans had got round them, and Lieutenant-Colonel Knox had to stop several of his men as they ran back. After a few words from Knox, they started to trot back the way they had come. As they went, Knox halted them, calmly made them smoke a cigarette and said, 'Now *walk* back'.

The situation on the maps was already beginning to look disquieting. Within four days the campaign in Holland had ended and the fate of Belgium was already sealed. Modern fortresses had fallen to glider-borne troops and two of the three vital bridges over the Albert Canal near Maastricht had been captured. The Belgian Air Force was powerless. They were flying Fiat biplanes with a machine-gun firing through the propellor, and when replacements came up they were even worse—Fairey Fireflies, built as early as 1929. With seven aeroplanes out of nine shot down in a vain attempt to destroy the bridges, Advanced Air Striking Force took on the job. Five Fairey Battles, slow three-seater machines, took off protected by six Hurricanes. The Hurricanes were immediately engaged by dozens of Messerschmitt 109s and all but one were destroyed, while of the Battles four were shot down over the targets and the fifth crashed on the return flight—but not before the Veldwezelt Bridge had been knocked out. By 12 May the bomber force of the AASF had shrunk to seventy-two, all of them desperately in need of servicing, and on 14 May, after a day to recuperate, seventy-one of them took off to attack the Sedan bridgehead in answer to a French demand for help. Forty of them never returned and the AASF was as good as finished.

The whole front began to crumble in a welter of indecision, and Horrocks, who had been brought up to believe French generals were the best strategists in Europe, began to wonder if that was right. On 16 May, Lord Gort, whose own front was holding firm against all German attacks against it, was ordered to withdraw to the line of the Escaut because the front of the French First Army on his right had been pierced. Because of the confused situation, there was not the slightest hope of reinforcing it and the French had to find a better defensive position. On his left the Belgians were endeavouring to form a line near Louvain, and the French Seventh Army, most of its strength lost in Holland, was having to fall back on Antwerp.

The British withdrawal began on the night of the 16th and by the same moonlight that helped them, Rommel smashed through the last French defences. The retreat to and the evacuation from Dunkirk had become inevitable.

'WE ALWAYS START WITH A RETREAT...'

That there was a disaster in the making very soon became obvious. The British Government had been incompetent and the Ministry of Supply had dawdled, and there was a feeling among the troops that Churchill should stuff his new government with crooks to get things done, because the honest men had not achieved much. Communications were also already going wrong, people were getting lost and troop carriers were failing to turn up, so that it was clear that if it came to a retreat it was going to be a matter of solid footslogging. There were already hundreds of refugees on the roads, pushing bicycles carrying blankets tied with string, and rumours of German parachutists everywhere, none of which seemed to be substantiated.

A wide search for them had been instituted by the 6th Black Watch after a sentry reported seeing parachutes coming down. As he soon afterwards reported seeing them go up again, his report was derided, but in fact, eighteen-year-old Gunner Bernard Hammond, with the 98th Field Regiment, Sussex Yeomanry, had a similar experience. Joining up because all his friends were joining, he had actually gone to war on a horse, and just before dawn on 10 May he had been awakened by the sound of aircraft overhead. He and his friends were all very green and when someone saw streaks of light coming down—which turned out to be tracer bullets from the aircraft—and shouted 'Gas', within seconds every man was standing covered from head to foot in gas cape and gas mask. A few days later, on sentry duty near the River Dyle, scared stiff and carrying a rifle he had never fired and scarcely knew how to load, he again saw white streaks in the sky—to his surprise, this time going upwards. Once more they turned out to be tracer bullets.

The Belgians were already reported to be cracking. The peasants the British met were looking glum, and in Brussels, where there were no British military police about, Basil Bartlett noticed that the mix-up was dreadful and the Belgian Army seemed to be evacuating itself as purposefully as the civilian population. Then they heard that Queen

Wilhelmina of the Netherlands was in Britain and that the Dutch had folded, and the thought of the Dutch ports in German hands caused shivers to run down his spine.

There was aerial activity now with a vengeance and they saw German planes chased by Hurricanes and were occasionally bombed, or showered with spent cartridges. Louvain was evacuated and refugees began to pour past, one old man on a bicycle commenting that he had done the same journey in 1914, but in half the time. The picture was becoming alarming and though British headquarters remained calm, news came that the Germans had broken through on the old battlefield at Sedan and that another breakthrough was beginning further north. The northern armies were being cut off.

Lance-Corporal Spike Mays, who as a reservist in the Royal Signals working for the Post Office had had the doubtful honour of receiving his recall to the colours on his own teleprinter, was in Cherbourg when the German breakthrough got under way. Having seen the Maginot Line and heard the oft-repeated postulations of the 'inmates', 'Ils ne passeront pas', he was astounded. Sent to Abbeville aerodrome with a radio van, he arrived just as the French took off in their stubby Bloc fighters to stop a group of German bombers. Erecting his aerial pole with its umbrella-like spokes, he was greeted by a young signals officer with the information that they expected to be bombed at any moment. Of the three Bloc fighters which had taken off only two returned, but a bomber was brought down among nearby trees. The French pilot was brought in on a haywain, 'his head so bullet-riddled . . .it looked like a mop of blood', and an ambulance brought in three young Germans. Two of them were taken to the guardroom, but when the third, a wounded tail gunner was lifted up, blood spurted from the bullet holes in a way that reminded Mays of his grandmother straining elderberries in her colander.

When, on the night of the 16th, orders came to the BEF to move back, they were surprised, but as Bartlett drove out of Brussels, apathetic Belgian soldiers were standing on corners, and outside the city there was a traffic jam five miles long. Behind them Brussels was burning and the German bombers were stoking the fire.

Unwillingly, the regiments went into reverse. In front of them, heading west, were the lines of communications troops, some still carrying the radios, football boots or tennis rackets they had collected during the winter. The fighting troops were doing very well, however, and Bartlett, very much the amateur brought up to believe that the top brass was none too bright, found himself agreeably surprised at the ability they were showing. The French he met were different. Their attitude now seemed to be less 'Ils ne passeront pas' than 'Good God, already?'

It had been the intention of the 7th Guards Brigade to hold the line of the Dyle, but Belgian Chasseurs refused to give place to them and insisted on manning a railway line in front which was a far weaker position than the canal. Behind them bridges were being prepared for demolition—under great difficulties, as hordes of people constantly wished to cross. After one fuse had been lit, in fact, a Belgian lorry full of troops and ammunition appeared out of the blue at high speed, to reach the centre of the bridge just as it went up. When the attack came during the night of 14–15 May, the Chasseurs disappeared at once and, with their flank now exposed, the Guards moved back to the canal positions they had first recommended.

Attached to the brigade was twenty-two-year-old Second Lieutenant Geoffrey Briggs, of the Coldstream. He had been commissioned as a regular soldier in 1937 and done his stint of public duties in London. In France he had been transferred to the brigade's Anti-Tank Company, a mixed unit of Grenadiers and Coldstream which had endured some shelling along the Albert Canal but had not been attacked by tanks. This was fortunate, he realised later on, because all they had were single-shot high-velocity 20mm French Hotchkisses which 'looked like motor scythes on wheels', and could stop a Bren carrier but not much else—just one degree better than the 'farcical' Boys anti-tank rifle, which, according to one officer, 'no one dared to touch'. Even the artillery's 18-pounders were not much help because there was little armour-piercing ammunition.

Here the Germans were stopped by sound troops using conventional fire power which was so accurate they thought they were facing a larger force than they were. The Guards considered they were doing rather well, in fact, and when they were ordered back on the night of the 16th they were very surprised. As they moved back Major R.B.R. Colvin, of the 2nd Grenadiers, was waiting on the Louvain road to check his battalion through as it retreated. 'It was a queer experience,' he wrote. '. . . one did not know if the first arrivals would be Guardsmen or Germans.' Two lambs with him bleated pathetically and all sorts of other animals turned up looking for someone to give them food and water.

The 1st Guards Brigade, in reserve to the 1st Division, was troubled by air attacks and the rumours of fifth columnists and parachutists. One man ran twice through their positions yelling 'Gas' and when a parachute floated down every Bren in the area opened fire. They all missed and it turned out to be a British pilot 'in an extremely bad temper', who broke his ankle on landing. When the cry of 'Gas' reached James Langley, he had just become separated from his gas mask and, though he knew it was impossible to suffocate himself voluntarily, he came very close to it in his efforts to hold his breath. He had remembered his company commander's words of wisdom: 'We always start a war with a retreat . . .' They *were* in retreat.

As the armies took up their new positions, in England people were beginning to realise the dangers of the German thrust. The BEF's main supply lines ran north-east through Amiens and Arras across the battlefields of World War I and, with the German spearheads posing a distinct threat to Amiens and reorganisation becoming vital, it was decided to base the BEF on the Channel ports, the responsibility of Dover Command under Vice–Admiral Bertram Ramsay.

Ramsay was a man of medium height with a quiet voice and an unemotional manner. Like Gort he was not popular and, indeed, was considered to have been a failure. He had had an undistinguished early career but, during World War I, had commanded HMS *Broke* of the Dover Patrol. In the post-war years he had moved steadily up the ladder and his efficiency as captain of *Royal Sovereign* brought him the appointment of Chief of Staff to the Home Fleet with the rank of rear-admiral. Unfortunately he clashed with his commanding officer and, after a single cruise, asked to be relieved, so that in 1938 he was placed on the retired list. His unquestioned ability brought him back and, at the time of the Munich crisis, because of his experience of the area, he was appointed to make an examination of Dover and its defences. He pulled no punches. The harbour had silted up, the port facilities were inadequate, the defences and communications dreadful. With Hitler appeased, Ramsay's services were again dispensed with, but a programme for the rehabilitation of Dover as a naval base was undertaken and Ramsay was given a dormant appointment in the event of hostilities to take command there. In September 1939 he had automatically become Flag Officer, Dover, and shortly afterwards, when the area became independent of the Nore Command, Vice-Admiral, Dover.

He had already had his first successes and his first losses. Many ships had escaped from Antwerp as the Germans advanced into Belgium and on 16 May 150,000 tons of oil were destroyed and the entrances to the docks and basins were blocked by demolition parties sent from Dover. With the German Navy temporarily *hors de combat* after Norway, the Germans could only respond with attacks by the Luftwaffe, but the destroyer *Valentine* was lost, and *Winchester* and *Westminster* were both badly damaged.

It was strange that, of the three men most heavily involved with the decisions of Dunkirk—Gort, Ramsay and Air Chief Marshal Sir Hugh Dowding, C-in-C, Fighter Command—none were popular. A shy man, Dowding had been known to his squadron in World War I as 'Starched Shirt' because he did not have the ability to communicate his enthusiasm or the affection he felt for his young pilots. He seemed aloof, quiet, unsmiling and apparently indifferent, but he was well aware of his responsibilities, and had noticed that as more squadrons of Hurricanes were fed into the fight across the Channel the RAF there had absorbed almost twelve of them. While Barratt, Gort and the French Prime Minister, Paul Reynaud, pleaded for more, Dowding decided they were merely being thrown away when they would be needed against the attacks on Britain which must surely follow. His arguments convinced the Cabinet and no more were sent. It was a decision that later led to recriminations between the Army and the Air Force, even to black eyes and, on one occasion after it was all over, a massive free-for-all. But as the Battle of Britain proved, it was the right decision.

So far, Gort's retreat had been accompanied by the Belgian Army on his left, and the French First Army on his right, but there was never any possibility of holding the line and on the night of the 17th the Allies fell back again. On the 18th they began a fresh withdrawal to the River Escaut but, since the French had inundated the Valenciennes area from the river to stop the Germans, the depth of water in front of the British was no more than 3ft, which hardly constituted a barrier. By this time the Germans had also reached St Quentin and by the 18th had captured Peronne, and people were laying odds against the BEF escaping. By the 19th they had crossed the Canal du Nord and were heading for the sea.

By this time, Gamelin—in the opinion of General Sir Edmund Ironside, Chief of Imperial General Staff, just 'a nice little man in a pair of well-cut breeches'—had lost control and been replaced by General Maxime Weygand, who had been Chief of Staff to Foch during World War I. There was still a measure of optimism in London, but to Gort it was fast becoming obvious that nothing could now stop the Germans. His lines of communication were cut and he was separated from his main supply dumps so that he realised he would now have to fight with what could be brought in by sea. With air support problematical, he also knew that the moment the Germans reached the coast the whole of his rear would be open and he began to face the possibility of a withdrawal to the Channel ports, something which would mean the abandonment of all his heavy guns and much equipment.

Also, he was losing faith in the French and, to make provision to guard his right flank, he organised a mixed force of armour and infantry under Major-General F.N. Mason-MacFarlane to cover the area from Maulde to Carvin on the La Bassée Canal. This was the first of a series of special forces which were to hold the German push to the north. Another force, under Major-General R.L. Petre, was organised for the defence of the Arras area. Despite this, however, no real front was established and the forces never held firm lines.

Just as it became clear that the French First Army at least would be able to hold its positions, the German breakthrough divided into two separate thrusts: one to the sea down the valley of the Somme, the other towards the Channel ports. As they advanced, the BEF and the troops in the north were slowly pressed into a pocket separate from the rest of the Allied line. Gort was still hoping for a link-up with the south, but when Ironside arrived from London with instructions that the BEF was to move on Amiens to the left of a new French army forming on the Somme, he realised that, heavily engaged already, short of ammunition, food and transport, such a move would mean abandoning the remaining dumps in Lille where the only petrol supply lay. The Belgians could not help and the French First Army already had its hands full, and it soon became clear that an attack southwards by the 5th and 50th Divisions under Major-General H.E. Franklyn, with what armour he could muster, was the only possible measure. More special forces were raised, one of them under Colonel C.M. Usher, who on his own initiative had already begun to organise measures to guard the approaches to Dunkirk.

As he returned to England, Ironside could do little else but write in his diary, 'God help the BEF'.

The confusion in France was incredible. Germans were appearing behind the British lines, and British units, apparently safely established, found their flanks in the air and themselves cut off. On one occasion an officer entering a house behind his own positions came face to face with a German who was as startled as he was. On another occasion a young subaltern and his driver, sent to find the Germans, found themselves heading directly towards a column of German motor cyclists. Reversing frantically and flattening themselves against a wall, they watched the column pass, followed by tanks. When they returned to report, they were not believed.

Private Leonard Green, of the Royal Army Service Corps (RASC), a young Cockney Jew only three months married, had always been under the impression that Hitler had been bluffing and was really as short of rubber and petrol as Allied propaganda had claimed. Now, trying with a party of men to reach Boulogne from Lille, he changed his mind. More than anything else it was the British soldiers burning or blowing up stores which convinced him. With their train crawling at a walking pace, the group split into smaller units of five or six men and changed trains from time to time by the simple expedient of walking along the line to the next one ahead. The confusion was absolute and on one occasion they saw military and civilian traffic running away in both directions at once, because no one knew where the front was.

Private Charles Cornford, a Territorial who was officers' mess cook for the 8th Worcesters, was riding in a furniture van containing all the mess equipment, drinks and officers' gear. On the way up, they had been urged on by unwilling French soldiers, waving their arms and yelling 'Bon, Tommee! You go on! Bang Bang!' Now, heading rearwards, they did not have the slightest idea what was happening. Taking a wrong turning and losing the convoy, they stopped outside a village to investigate and, peeping through a window, were horrified to find themselves staring at Germans. Creeping away and turning round, they then ran into a cloud of French cavalrymen who blocked the road with their horses and, to pass them, the top-heavy furniture van was driven down a steep bank, leaning over at an incredible angle.

The bewildering part was that while the British remained in the dark about the Germans, the Germans always seemed to know exactly where the British were. As Sergeant A. Gough's unit of Royal Engineers took shelter in a wood on a hill, the dust stirred up by their vehicles was spotted by a German observation balloon and almost immediately the wood was covered with shrapnel shells that exploded 'like the crack of doom'. Gough saw men, many of them young conscripted soldiers, running about ripped to ribbons, and others lying on their faces with their backs and legs slashed. As the survivors crawled over the hill through the trees, Gough gave a fireman's lift to a driver with a torn thigh. By now there were only about 100 men left of the original 300 and only about six or seven of their vehicles were fit for service.

Ordered to Halle, south of Brussels, to blow bridges behind the retreating army, Gough arrived in the middle of a flood of refugees just as four German fighters came over with their guns blazing. Grabbing two children, he dived for the ditch. The parents were killed in the attack with dozens of others. He had brought plenty of explosive, however, and the shock wave as he blew the Halle bridge 'almost wrecked the town'.

Second Lieutenant Alan Street, a Regular soldier in the Royal Army Ordnance Corps (RAOC), found himself seeking billets at a Belgian chateau. The place was deserted except for the Belgian baroness, whom they discovered in the kitchen peeling potatoes. Her chief concern was with the fact that she should greet them with dirty hands and with the fate of two spaniel puppies she owned. She begged them to take the two dogs with them and, since his company commander had a bulldog he had brought from England, Street agreed to take one while his sergeant took the other.

The BEF was now in an area which had been fought over again and again in history, and famous regiments found themselves passing old battlefields where they had distinguished themselves in past campaigns. The 6th Black Watch, its carriers crowded and some of its men already on bicycles or on foot, passed close to Fontenoy where they had fought their first action in 1745; and close to Waterloo, where the regiment had faced the French in 1815, were the 4th Oxford and Buckinghamshire Light Infantry, with the 48th Division. As the division approached Tournai with the 2nd Division, the route became choked with civilian vehicles, among them a travelling circus, and as the Luftwaffe caught them, horrified soldiers saw wounded elephants rampaging to safety and a team of white horses dragging away the limp body of a girl. As the divisions separate, the 48th's vehicles became strung out and, near Tournai, a smartly dressed Sapper major appeared, to marshal them into a closer formation. It seemed no coincidence that as he disappeared the Luftwaffe returned. The Ox and Bucks lost 48 men and the Gloucesters almost 200.

With the 1st East Surreys, who had crossed the border at Hallouin and gone into action at Oudenaarde beyond the Escaut, on the site of one of Marlborough's battles, was Private William Loveland, a Regular soldier who had served in India. One of his friends, Private William Hersey, was very worried about his wife, a French girl from Tourcoing, whom he had married only three weeks before. He was anxious to get back to warn her to be ready to leave, but so far there had been no time, and he had to keep hoping that the opportunity would arise as they pulled back. As they lay in slit trenches, Loveland noticed that enemy fire was coming from a wood on their left which should have been occupied by a British battalion, and a few of the young conscripts who were with him began to grow anxious. Sergeant 'Taffy' Cole, however, standing upright between the trenches firing a Bren from the hip, was showing splendid indifference and shooting a lot of Germans.

'Come on, Sarge,' one of the boys urged. 'Let's get out of here!'

Cole eyed him coldly. 'You shut up,' he advised, 'or I'll shoot you, too!'

Oudenaarde was full of troops and civilians, and as they were caught by the Luftwaffe, a young Territorial artillery officer with the 92nd Field Regiment, who wrote an account of Dunkirk under the *nom de plume*, 'Gun Buster', saw what happened. Just as he arrived on the outskirts twenty or thirty German bombers appeared. 'We found ourselves gazing in amazement,' he wrote, '. . . the charming little town had suddenly disappeared and in its place was a cloud of reddish dust and black smoke, pierced here and there by great leaping flames. . . Hardly had we begun to hear the thud-thud of the bombs before all was silent. The raiders had vanished.'

So had Oudenaarde, and only a curious pinkish haze marked where it had stood. Buildings were heaps of bricks and mortar. Beds had been hurled out of windows and hung over the pavements, houses had been neatly sliced in half, and the reddish dust that came from thousands of pulverised roof tiles was settling over everything. A few women crept out of cellars, grey with terror and sobbing hysterically, and by the river three little girls knelt with the palms of their hands pressed frantically together, praying in front of a wooden calvary, all the time under the shower of red dust, 'like a fine rain of blood'.

Falling back to the Escaut with the Coldstream, James Langley was placed in charge of a bridge. Warned not to destroy it with half the BEF on the wrong side, his chief fear was not the Germans but his company commander's wrath if he blew it too early. Occupying a small chateau at Pecq, he was awaiting the Germans when a voice called out, 'Hi! Can any of your fellows over there swim? I'm not very good at it and I have a wounded man with me.' If the Germans had waited three seconds more they would have wiped out Langley's whole platoon, but they fired too soon and managed to kill only one and wound two others. Fortunately, in the scramble for cover, the Bren gunner kept his head and silenced the German fire.

The Germans then tried the old dodge of raising a helmet on a stick to draw the British snipers' fire. After a while the single helmet became two and then three, and it finally dawned on Langley that one of the helmets contained a head and eyes which were taking advantage of the indifference of the Guardsmen to the trick, to spy out the land. The helmets came up only once more. Even now the Germans had not finished, and when four pairs of Germans appeared, each carrying a stretcher draped with a Red Cross flag and led by two Germans without rifles, it was assumed they were attempting to recover their dead. But what had been thought to be a groundsheet suddenly started to swell into an air-inflated rubber boat. That was another ploy that did not work.

As the stretcher bearers arrived to carry away the British dead, Langley saw with horror one of the 'corpses', who had the point of a bullet sticking out of his forehead, suddenly open his eyes and ask for a cigarette. He complied with the request but the man died. Throughout the day, there was sniping and desultory shelling which killed and wounded a number of sheep, horses and cows, one of which, maddened with pain, jumped into the moat and swam round it, mooing mournfully until Langley finished it off with his rifle.

Also at Pecq, the 3rd Grenadier Guards were trying to put in an attack through a cornfield. Guardsman Albert Eldridge had joined up in 1930 at the age of seventeen and had often cried himself to sleep at the harsh discipline. That same discipline now looked very different, because it meant that whatever happened there was always someone to take command. Even when there were no officers or NCOs left, they all knew who was senior soldier and automatically did as he said. On 21 May they had put in an attack with the Coldstream and the Hampshires, losing three of their officers, and now they found that as soon as they entered the western edge of the cornfield they came under very heavy fire. While they lay low they were fairly safe but as soon as they raised their heads to fire back or tried to emerge, a stream of bullets raked the corn tops. Realising there were two main groups of Germans, the Grenadiers were divided into two parties. Eldridge's right-hand party made some progress before they were overwhelmed by the fire and three of their officers were killed, including the Duke of Northumberland who tried to use his carriers as tanks. The left-hand group struggled to a poplar-covered ridge and one of Eldridge's friends, Lance-Corporal Harry Nicholls, the battalion's heavyweight boxing champion, advanced with Guardsman Nash, who was feeding him with ammunition, firing with a Bren from the hip. Twice wounded, he managed to reach the ridge and opened a devastating fire on the Germans until he was hit again and collapsed. For his action he was awarded the VC, thought at the time to be posthumous, though he was later found to be a prisoner in a German hospital.

Meanwhile, to the south, Rommel had turned towards the sea. But the German Command had been expecting counter-attacks from the moment they had broken through and now when Franklyn's move came from Arras its vigour and élan upset Rommel's judgement. He felt there were five British divisions opposite him though, in fact, the attack was delivered by a mere seventy-four tanks—most of them in desperate need of overhaul—supported by two battalions of infantry, with small numbers of French light tanks on the right. Although the attack was halted, the Germans had been shocked by its ferocity and began to fear for their isolated armoured spearheads.

If the Germans could not at this point see what was happening, Gort could. The new head of the Allied Forces, Weygand, who had only recently arrived from Syria, seemed totally unaware of the true situation and no direct contact was ever established between him and Gort, whose conference now came to the conclusion that it was impossible to go on holding the line of the Escaut. The only alternative was a withdrawal to the old frontier positions to take advantage of the fortifications which had been built during the winter. The Belgians were to pull back to the Lys.

Planning for an evacuation had already started in England and now Gort's staff began work on a plan of their own. Arras still held, however, a pall of smoke thick over the city as the battle raged, and special forces were taking up positions along the Aa-La Bassée-Haut Deale Canal Line, while the French First Army was still hanging on, and, at 9 am the next morning, as the draft plan for the evacuation was completed, Gort's staff were informed it was not needed. A new French plan for an attack southwards had been originated by Weygand to join an attack north to cut off the Germans.

Unfortunately Weygand's orders were almost incoherent and there was not the slightest chance of an attack with the eight divisions suggested. When General Georges, the French Commander North-East Front, proved equally vague, General Blanchard, who had succeeded Billotte—killed in a road accident on his way back from Gort's conference the previous day—simply did not bother to take any action.

The armies were now streaming back through the pillboxes and trenches of the earlier war, passing iron corkscrews which had once held barbed wire but now supported fencing to keep cows from straying. For miles there was not a tree more than 12 feet high, where in that earlier war the woods had been blasted to nothing. They were still fighting well and without panic and at one point when supporting artillery spotted a mass of German infantry and blazed away at it, they were reprimanded by a Guards subaltern. 'You might have let them come a bit nearer,' he said bitterly. 'We were laying for them with machine–guns.'

The roads, which before had contained hundreds of civilian refugees, now contained thousands, all terrified. Villages were left empty and the 6th Black Watch, forced back as they became enveloped by swarms of attackers, saw all the signs of panic as they passed through Peteghem. Cigarettes had burned themselves out on tables in bars, glasses had been abandoned half-drained, and a game of draughts left half-finished.

Caught in the columns of retreating traffic, Intelligence Captain Basil Bartlett slept with others in an 'insanitary heap' in an abandoned house in Sweveghem. The muddle was appalling. There were abandoned animals, unmilked cows, songbirds dead in cages, rabbits in hutches, dogs and cats dead in back rooms. Whenever they could, the sentimental British soldiers set them free.

At Werwicq on 23 May, they found no gunfire, but the following day communications with Lille broke down and in Roubaix and Tourcoing cellars were being prepared for refugees from the frontier villages. French officers doing the requisitioning said a battle at Cambrai was imminent. 'We must not despair', one of them said, and Bartlett decided it was the first optimistic comment he had ever heard from the French on any subject at all.

Also trying to reach Lille were the 6th Royal Sussex who left Rouen by train with the 7th Battalion and the 2nd/6th East Surreys. The order of moving showed the 6th in front but, since the 7th were ready first, they left first. Just as they entered Amiens, with the trains 200 yards apart, the leading train was hit by a tremendous salvo of bombs which caused dozens of casualties, including eight officers.

The 4th and 5th Royal Sussex, already engaged in the fighting, had been left on high ground near Anseghem. Private Michael Morphy, who joined them as they were forced back, had been tea planting in Ceylon when war broke out and had paid his own fare home to join the Army. It was an indication of the attitude in Britain at that time

that he found it extraordinarily difficult, and only managed it on his
third attempt because he met a recruiting sergeant who came from his
home town. After only six weeks' training he had gone with others
to France as reinforcements and now they entrained at Rouen for
Lillers near Lille. Because he could speak schoolboy French, he was
put on a roadblock to sort the spies or parachutists dressed as nuns
from the refugees.

When the 5th Battalion appeared in lorries, he was wearing a
Balaclava helmet despite the heat and one of the officers swore at
him. 'Take that bloody thing off and get aboard the lorry,' he was
ordered. He presumed he was now part of the 5th Battalion.

At Lille, they were billeted for a while in the local lunatic asylum.
Morphy still had no idea what was going on and when next day they
marched on 'a circular tour' and returned to the asylum without doing
anything, he could only assume they had been attached to the asylum
'to double its strength'. Eventually, however, they were fallen in as a
battalion and ended up on Hazebrouck Ridge. As they marched up
the reverse slope towards the enemy, the order of march was B, A
and C Companies, but for some reason they were halted and A took
the lead. As they marched through a village on the ridge and down
the other side, terrific firing broke out from Germans in ditches on
either side of the road and A Company was almost wiped out.

Moving up to the village, the rest of them found a Middlesex
heavy machine-gun unit holding it, with German tanks in a field of
tall corn beyond. Ricochets were striking the road and whizzing past
Morphy with a 'pssh-brrmm' noise. In innocence, he asked 'What
are all those bloody catherine wheels doing?' Machine-guns from
the tanks opened up and they dived for the ditch. After a while,
as they crouched there, the tanks moved on, and in the quiet an
old man, his wife and daughter appeared wheeling a bicycle with
all their belongings on it. The old lady found walking difficult and
when they tried to put her on the bicycle she fell off with the load
of household goods. Assisted by the soldiers, she was placed on the
handlebars with her back to the road and, festooned with packages,
finally disappeared to cheers.

The Sussex men remained there for some time and, as they
waited, shelling started and farms and windmills across the road
started to burn. Houses on their own side followed and Captain
Tim Hole made a point of standing up and 'doing a 1914 act to set
an example of what a good officer should be'. It had a tremendous
effect on the morale of his young troops, but the men on either side

of Morphy began to grow jumpy and he found it infectious. By this time the sky was full of flares and Very lights and when Hole asked for a runner to go with him, Morphy volunteered with alacrity.

Gunner Hammond, bundled back with the 98th Field Regiment, had also reached Hazebrouck, where one of their 18-pounders was taken for the defence of one of six bridges as an anti-tank gun. On 24 May, with the front broken, the appropriated gun was dug in on the flank where it bore the brunt of an attack by eleven tanks. It knocked out one and damaged another, but was drenched in fire which killed or wounded all the remaining members of the detachment. Though badly wounded, Sergeant Mordin kept the gun firing until its ammunition trailer blew up. It was young Hammond, willing but still scared stiff, who brought up a tractor and amazingly the gun was dragged away. Inspired by this effort, the clerks and batmen holding the northern outskirts of the town clung on and, with the assistance of a few Belgians, managed to force the panzers to withdraw late in the evening.

The Germans were still making important advances, however, and considerable losses were being sustained by the British as the BEF tried to disengage itself. Ammunition, equipment and ordnance stores were already in short supply and the food situation was so precarious they were put on half rations. In fact, supplies varied from unit to unit, Montgomery even driving a herd of cattle on the hoof.

By this time, the Germans had cut a great swath through the Allied forces. Reaching the sea, they had besieged Boulogne, which was already almost finished. Calais was to be besieged before the day was out and, with the panzers across the canal line at St Omer, Arras was now outflanked. From Vimy Ridge, that rise in the Flanders plain made famous in World War I, it was possible to see towards the town, where the Welsh Guards, a few stout-hearted Territorials, Sappers and tank men were clinging on like leeches. At night the whole area was lit up with the flashes of bursting bombs and shells and the flames of two big fires. Tracer shells made Disney-like designs in the sky and Very lights burst in red, green, blue or yellow. When a white rocket soared up the watchers knew that it was to indicate to German HQ that some new objective had been captured.

Then, during the evening of 23 May, the situation changed dramatically. By this time, German General Gerd von Runstedt, commanding Army Group A in the south, and lost 50 per cent of his armour to enemy action and wear and tear and, with the terrain beyond the canal in front of him seamed by dykes and flooded areas, he was convinced he would have to pay heavily for any further advance. Thinking in terms also of a future attack across the Somme into the heart of France, he gave the order to halt and regroup. Equally worried for the same reasons, Hitler confirmed the order. It was Reichsmarschall Hermann Göring's vanity that had persuaded him. After the victories over the Polish and French air forces, Adolf Galland, the German fighter plane leader, said he was more than ever a partisan of the Stuka, and General Walter Warlimont, Chief of Operations at German GHQ, heard him say 'My Luftwaffe will complete the encirclement and . . . close the pocket from the air'.

In fact, the Germans had nothing to fear. The fight around Arras had destroyed the last of the British armour. Second Lieutenant P.A.L. Vaux, with the 4th Tanks, having been sent off by his colonel to try to encourage the French to come to their assistance, returned to see twenty or so of his regiment's vehicles in a valley, among them the colonel's. Trying to make contact by radio, he received no reply, so he moved nearer, thinking it odd that none of the tanks were moving. Then he noticed their guns were pointing at all angles, and that a lot of them had their turret hatches open with men lying half-in and half-out. With a shock he realised that all twenty had been knocked out by German guns.

Like the British, the French had little left that was worthwhile. Gort's special forces were also almost finished, though they had done magnificently. Composed of every branch of the British Army and very often lacking signals, supplies and transport, they had managed to block German intentions at every major point. Now, however, with the Germans flooding past them, Gort had to give the Arras garrison orders to withdraw. Immediately Weygand burst into a tirade of fury that the British were forcing him to abandon his great plan.

For the men involved in the fighting, it had been a traumatic time. It was a soldiers' battle everywhere, the fog of uncertainty as thick as the mist at Inkerman, and the Army was saved from disintegration as much as anything by its warrant officers, non-commissioned officers, Regular soldiers and time-expired men brought back from Civvy Street. Because they knew their job, many of the Territorials and young conscripts owed their lives to them.

All round them anarchic bands of French soldiers from Blanchard's and Corap's armies were roaming across the lines of communication, looting and drinking. Officers who tried to take control were shot by them and, to justify their desertion, they spread stories of thousands

of German tanks and parachutists, which only added to the demorali-
sation. The thing Horrocks remembered most of all was the exhaustion
and the shame he felt as he headed back through white-faced crowds
of silent Belgians. They had driven up so jauntily and now they were
scurrying back with their tails between their legs. The infuriating
thing was that they had not been beaten, and all he could do was
mutter 'Don't worry. We'll come back'. As it happened, he did, as
the general in command when Brussels was liberated.

The roads were crammed with refugees by this time, in long crawling
columns 'like black treacle' all pressing in one direction, driven on by
terror, without order and without control. They received no instructions and were never controlled by police, so that they wandered in
dumb panic, bombed and machine-gunned, imploring the troops to
tell them a safe route away from the Germans. They rode on bicycles,
in carts, traps and old cars, some of which, judging by the straw and
dust on them, had rested for years in barns until this moment and
now struggled to reach safety. Often the pedestrians carried nothing
but a blanket tied over their shoulders or pushed their belongings in
wheelbarrows, prams, even children's trolleys. Some of the women
were clothed for the journey, others struggled along in smart hats,
fur coats and dainty footwear. Trying to force a passage, often in the
opposite direction, were tanks, guns, motor cycles and trucks, both
British and French, their weary drivers falling asleep whenever they
were halted. As the column moved on again, the military police went
round waking them up, as often as not by banging on their helmets
with revolvers.

When the Stukas came, there was a wild rush for safety and in one
village an artillery unit, searching for gun pits they had dug earlier,
found them packed with dead and dying men, women and children
who had taken shelter there. At Carvin, near the La Bassée Canal,
the bodies of sixty young girls, pupils from a bombed school, were
seen lying on the pavement in the moonlight.

All too often the soldiers had no idea where the Germans were.
Regularly under fire, Sergeant Gough, of the Engineers, reached a
bridge guarded by a man with a Bren. Tossing up with his companion
whether to approach it along the road or across a field, he had the
decision taken out of his hands when a shell landed on the bridge
and man and gun vanished.

Picking up men from pre-selected places, he now headed for the
canal to blow the lock gates, only to come under fire from what he
had to assume were fifth columnists. Thousands of refugees were

trying to cross the canal but, with his orders to stop them, Gough had to watch stony-faced as old women and children got down on their knees to beg to be allowed to pass. He and his men blew the lock gates the following day to flood the countryside.

Continuing northwards, placing booby traps on houses and cross-roads as they went, about 3 am in the first light of the day he saw a head approaching his party just above the mist, as if its owner were riding in a scout car or a weapon carrier. They were mixed now with other units and it was an indication of the confusion that they had no idea what he was and grew more than ever certain he was a German. 'I don't trust him,' a tank sergeant said. 'He's going to have it.' The man was killed but turned out to be a Belgian despatch rider on a motor cycle.

The congestion round Armentières, which had been set alight by the Luftwaffe, was appalling. To add the final note of madness the lunatics had been let out of the local asylum and were standing at the roadside with inane grins on their faces and saliva dribbling from their chins. Nineteen-year-old Trooper Gillam, of the 12th Lancers, was in the town with a group of men in a 3-tonner from B Echelon to bury one of their casualties in the cemetery. They had to break open the gates in the dark and dig the grave themselves and while they were doing it an attractive French girl flung herself across the body, weeping and waving a photograph. Gillam could only assume that the dead man made her think of someone she knew.

When they returned, the regiment had been scattered and they pulled off the main road into a wood. As they did so, Gillam stumbled over a trip wire connected to a shotgun set for poachers and was hit by seventy or eighty pellets. They were 'up his nose, in his ears and all round his backside' and his friends picked them out in the kitchen of a French house, laughing far more than Gillam, who could not sit down for a long time. He considered himself wounded more times than any man in the Army. Picking up rations, they made stews and took them up to the fighting troops, but then the fighting troops moved back and B Echelon found they were between the front line and the enemy.

By the time Captain Basil Bartlett managed to struggle into Lille, there were few people left in the place and many of the police were drunk. At the only bar they found open, the furious proprietor was dancing with rage and shouting 'We'll beat them, we'll beat them!' In the same vicinity was Gunner Donald Webb, a Territorial with a 25-pounder battery of the 91st Field Regiment, Royal Artillery. They had been bombed near Halle by Messerschmitts which had shot down a Lysander, whose gunner had been brought to their first–aid post. He was only eighteen years old and had lost a finger. His tunic was opened from top to bottom by bullets and he was shuddering from shock.

Stopping at an estaminet, they saw a farmer wringing his hands and moaning 'La guerre est finie'. Asked which way they were going, they realised they did not know and fell back on the excuse all the British were giving—'Don't worry. We'll be back.' Passing through Tournai, where every house seemed to be in flames, they saw infantry taking up positions in the old 1914–18 trenches to await the German attacks and, by now almost cut off, they were ordered to break north. Just as the movement was about to start, 'the whole German Air Force' came down—Heinkels, Dorniers and Stukas. The bridge over the Scarpe was demolished but the engineers managed to throw another one across and the column headed for it. In the confusion, however, Webb's battery was overlooked. They heard the infantry pulling out in the darkness but they were still stationary next day and still firing when British-built Gladiator fighters came over. Thinking it was the RAF to the rescue, they cheered, only to find themselves on the receiving end of a bombing raid, and they learned that the aircraft were captured Dutch machines. They were beginning by this time to think they were being deliberately sacrificed to hold up the Germans, but they finally received the order to pull out. Everything had gone deathly quiet, Webb noticed, and he decided it was a bad sign. Sure enough, as they got their vehicles and guns on to the road, the Germans started firing on the village, and they left in a flurry of explosions.

By 25 May what was left of the area held by the armies of the north was roughly the shape of an inverted boot. The sole was the Belgian shore, the toe lay at the estuary of the Scheldt and the heel lay at Gravelines. The back of the boot was the Canal Line running up to Valenciennes, the instep the old frontier defences manned again by the BEF. From there to the toe they were manned by the Belgian Army. Under the circumstances, the draft plan for evacuation was brought out again.

The western battle had died down, but the Germans were still pecking at the Canal Line when, on the 25th, General Sir John Dill, Vice-Chiefrea of Imperial General Staff, arrived from London. He was clearly dissatisfied with Gort's generalship but he left sufficiently convinced by what was happening to reject out of hand any further attack southward. With the Belgians on the point of collapse, Gort studied the situation. Weygand, Georges, Blanchard and the British

Government had all ordered him to attack south, but deciding it could not be done, he ordered the 5th and 50th Divisions to abandon their preparations and move at once to cover a gap developing between the British and the Belgian armies.

It was against all his instincts and against all the orders he had received, and he knew it would mean the end of the attack south, but that decision, taken after hours of thought, saved the BEF. Half an hour later a signal arrived to say that a gap had been broken in the line and that the Belgians had used up their last reserves and could not hope to close it.

OPERATION DYNAMO

Naval Headquarters at Dover were set in deep galleries, hewn in the chalk of the east cliff below Dover Castle by French prisoners during the Napoleonic Wars. The nerve centre was a gallery ending in an embrasure at the cliff face, which was used as an office by Admiral Ramsay. Behind were a succession of small rooms and beyond them a large space known as the Dynamo Room, which was to give its name to the operation Ramsay was to initiate.

By this time, Antwerp and Flushing had been blocked. The possibility of using Calais, Boulogne and even small ports like Gravelines and Etaples to remove troops from France had been considered, but at this point thoughts still concerned only lines of communications soldiers, base units, hospital staffs and other odd personnel. The evacuation of very large forces was still considered unlikely. Even on 22 May nothing in the nature of a 'panic' evacuation was contemplated, but by the morning of the 23rd from the windows of Ramsay's office it was possible to see the shell bursts of the attack on Boulogne and, with the coast of France clear in the brilliant sunshine, the prepared plan was seen already to be shattered.

It was clear that, though the Germans held the coast from near Calais to the mouth of the Somme, there was little to fear at sea in that direction because they could not bring anything through the Channel, and the speed of the disaster was such that few U-boats could be closed up quickly enough to have any effect. The eastern flank, however, was very vulnerable because German E-boats were known to be operating from the Scheldt. Of course, the need to guard the Channel did not in any way diminish the need to watch Norway, the Mediterranean and the Atlantic, but in the end the Admiralty managed to find forty destroyers for Dunkirk— a quarter of its destroyer strength—while also available were ferry steamers, ships which for years had been plying chiefly between France and Britain, a lot of flat-bottomed Dutch schuits, or skoots, which had escaped to England, and a fleet of drifters and coasters.

On Gort's orders, the 'useless mouths' of the Army were already being evacuated from Calais, Boulogne and Dunkirk. With the BEF, the tail of non-fighting soldiers that lies behind a modern army was larger than normal because the BEF had been considered to be only the nucleus of what would eventually be a great British army in France, and behind the line were administrative, development and training units designed to handle the large numbers of men expected to be raised by conscription. Those on the fringe of the battle had been swept up by Gort's special forces but the rest were only an unnecessary target and a drain on supplies.

Removing them, however, was far from easy. By 20 May ships endeavouring to supply the BEF or tow home damaged vessels were already being bombed and by 22 May the hospital carriers moving wounded from Dunkirk found that the air raids were increasing. The 20th Guards Brigade, which had been landed at Boulogne on the 21st, found the quays littered with abandoned vehicles and the French and Belgian units there lacking in discipline. They dug in on the perimeter and, assisted by the guns of *Vimy*, *Wild Swan*, *Whitshed*, and *Keith*, which fired at what targets they could find among the German tanks, guns and motorised formations, held an attack by General Heinz Guderian's 22nd Panzers. During the air attacks that developed, however, *Keith*'s captain was killed and *Vimy*'s fatally wounded. The French lost the destroyer *Orage*, and *Frondeur* was severely damaged.

With the situation deteriorating, the troops had to be extricated again and *Whitshed* went in as the Guards formed up and marched with parade ground precision to the harbour. *Vimiera* was on the point of leaving when she was rushed by civilians and French and Belgian soldiers, but 1,000 Guardsmen also managed to reach her and, with 1,400 people on board, she escaped, although the French destroyer *Fougueux* was damaged and *Chacal* was left in a sinking condition.

There was no hope whatsoever of escape from Calais. The late Airey Neave, MP, then a troop commander in a searchlight battery, considered to be non-fighting troops, had been left behind when the 'useless mouths' had been evacuated, and found himself and his men, with a variety of elderly weapons, attached to the 60th Rifles and told to 'fight like bloody hell'. Gunner James West's unit of heavy ack-ack, which had been firing for five days as anti-tank guns with 66lb HE shells and guessed sights and fuses, were told to blow up their guns and retreat to the docks where they also joined rifle regiments to fight as infantrymen. Ordered to continue the struggle to the last man, they were so exhausted they felt no emotion whatsoever.

As the town fought to the end, Ramsay's destroyers endeavoured to carry out supporting bombardments. Indeed, they were still firing over Gunner West's head as he sat with other newly captured prisoners on the promenade with his hands up. During this work *Wessex* was sunk and *Vimiera* and the Polish destroyer *Burza* were badly damaged. By Sunday 26 May the Navy had lost four destroyers in forty-eight hours.

Sunday the 26th was a National Day of Prayer and people in England streamed to church to pray for their beleaguered army. The beleaguered army took the view that the time might have been better spent doing something to help them. To be fair, the people at home had no real knowledge of the extent of the disaster, and they went about their business largely as usual, going out for Sunday drives, playing cricket or planning their holidays. Dover, nearer to the great events, was already working at full speed. Sixteen ships lay at Admiralty Pier where there were normally eight berths for cross-Channel steamers. They would soon become eighteen and then twenty. They all had to be handled by tugs and as soon as they came alongside and the soldiers had disembarked they were hauled out to refuel and return. At one of the buoys in the harbour an oil tanker was moored, and refuelling alongside her were destroyers or cross-Channel ships, all of which also had to be moved by tugs. When they came to HMS *Whitshed* and *Vimy*, their crews were so tired that the tug men moved the ships without them. On 25 May, hospital ships were still trying to lift the wounded from Dunkirk under heavy bombing. This bombing had destroyed water mains, and with the deliberate flooding round the town, brackish water was seeping into the wells, so that an urgent signal was sent to England for water boats.

As the disaster in France unfolded, it was becoming clear to the planners that hopes would have to rest on Dunkirk and its beaches, which stretched from Gravelines in the west through Malo-les-Bains, Bray Dunes and La Panne to Nieuport just across the Belgian frontier in the east, a matter of 25 miles. Wide, flat, level and largely featureless, these beaches were dirty grey in colour and striped with black. Offshore were numerous sandbanks and over the sand stretched an occasional low breakwater. The dunes behind were heavily contoured and tufted with marram grass. There were no piers, and the beaches, shelving out a long way to deep water, were totally exposed to northerly winds.

Behind the rash of tasteless houses that fringed the sand, the fields stretched to the horizon, more Dutch than French in appearance, while the ground was cut up by canals and irrigation ditches, the roads running on raised embankments alongside to provide the only ridges. It was difficult country for armour, because it had no cover, a water obstacle every quarter mile and fields that were already flooding as breaches were blown in the dykes.

Dunkirk itself, the third port of France, had a fine modern harbour with seven dock basins, four dry docks and five miles of quays going deep into the town. The docks had already been rendered useless by the bombing. Only of any use were the West Mole, projecting from the oil storage area, the East Mole, projecting from the ancient fortifications 1,400 yards into the sea, and the guiding jetty to the new basin. Of these, the East Mole—nothing but a narrow plankway with rails of timber, above which piles projected to make posts to which ships could moor in an emergency—was to prove vital.

That morning, Gort received a telegram from Anthony Eden, now Secretary of State for War in place of Hore-Belisha, which admitted that the French offensive from the Somme was no longer possible and that it was his duty to fight his way to the beaches and ports east of Gravelines. Gort's reply made no bones about the situation '. . . I must not conceal from you,' he said, 'that a great part of the BEF and its equipment will inevitably be lost even in the best circumstances.'

The eastern flank was still holding, however, because the main weight of the German Army was concentrated in the south and Lieutenant–General Alan Brooke's Second Corps, reinforced by the 5th and 50th Divisions, was well established behind the old frontier defences. But despite Von Runstedt's 'standstill' order, fighting had not ceased in the west, and as Gort struggled to bring sense to the confusion, he received a second telegram from Eden which ended with the information that there was no longer any course open to him but to fall back to the coast. At 6.57 pm the Admiralty made the signal, 'Operation Dynamo to commence'. In fact, Ramsay had already started the flow of ships to Dunkirk and the first of them were embarking troops as the signal arrived.

The Navy's experience of evacuation was not small. Among others, it had evacuated Sir John Moore's army from Corunna in 1808, and at the beginning of 1916 had extricated an army from the Dardanelles under the worst possible conditions. Nevertheless, Ramsay's task was not easy. With barely a flotilla of destroyers, he had to make safe the area through which the evacuation was to take place, protect the east, cover the evacuation routes, provide counter-bombardment against German batteries near Calais and anti-aircraft protection for his ships, sweep the approach channels and the area off Dunkirk, organise the traffic and provide a rescue service. He had 35 personnel ships, 6 coasters, 16 wooden and steel barges, 40 Dutch skoots, and 32 other ships. Late that evening, London informed him it was imperative for Dynamo to be implemented with the greatest vigour, with a view to lifting up to 45,000 men of the BEF in two days, at the end of which the evacuation was expected to be brought to an end by enemy action.

It was on this difficult day that Captain Basil Bartlett, after his long trek from Brussels, began to head for the coast. Indeed, as the BEF became confined in an increasingly small area, there seemed nowhere else to go. Constantly bombed, his men were exhausted but they remained remarkably philosophical, and at 11 pm they started to make for Furnes, 15 miles from Dunkirk, having first taken the precaution of stuffing their vehicles with what food they could get.

Moving from the aerodrome at Abbeville, Signals Lance-Corporal Spike Mays had reached Le Pin where he parked his van near a French light ack-ack battery. The French were so worried about the Luftwaffe he and his driver were ordered to refrain from smoking even in daylight, lie flat and speak only in whispers. They regularly heard German bombers overhead but no shots were fired until all hell broke loose against a Dakota carrying British markings. It was shot down.

Lieutenant-Colonel R. W. Strudwick, commanding the 3rd Super Heavy Artillery, had huge 12in howitzers for which each shell weighed about 750lb. His battery was one-third Territorials and the rest Regulars or reservists, all experienced, steady soldiers. Ordered to move to Abbeville, they had wandered about until 22 or 23 May when, heading towards Calais, they bumped into a group of men cycling towards them who looked French but turned out to be ex-British soldiers who had been tending World War I cemeteries.

'It's no good up there,' they said. 'Calais has fallen!'

Abruptly changing direction, they crossed the bridge at Watten on the Aa Canal just before it was blown, and, immediately becoming part of Usherforce, were ordered to fight as infantry.

The confusion was now at its height. In Ploegsteert, known to the men of 1914–18 as 'Plug Street', Acting Unpaid Lance-Corporal Donald Warner, of the Military Police, found himself trying to sort out differing streams of traffic as he stood on point duty. As the vehicles passed, questions were shot at him from all sides. 'Where's the 54th?' 'Which direction did the 7th Battalion take?' He did not know any of the answers and, although he was keeping the traffic moving, he did not have enough information to send anybody in any particular direction.

Second Lieutenant Street and his sergeant, who still had the two spaniel puppies with them, passed farms which were totally deserted except for chained guard dogs savage with hunger. They could not get near them and even if they had been able to they had no food to give them and the orders were to shoot them. At one small town, a Frenchman who owned a small brewery gave them the key, telling them to take as much as they could so the Germans would not get it. There was nothing they could do about that either. At Neuve Chapelle, as Gunner William Bain came through with 'Gun Buster's' unit, the 92nd Field Regiment, a farmer offered them his pigs, begging them to eat them so they would not fall into German hands. They also did not have the time.

Private Loveland, of the East Surreys, was now across the Escaut. His friend, Hersey, finally given permission to collect his wife, had vanished on a bicycle to find her. Among the rearguard at the tail of the retreat was Driver/Mechanic Lloyd George Fitsell, of the 2nd Royal Sussex. They had been rushed up to fill a gap in the 131st Brigade's front and had dug in behind the railway line near Anseghem. Near them were the Buffs, the Queens and the West Kents and they were on the receiving end of a tremendous shelling. They held the German rushes but there were dead cattle everywhere and as they crouched behind sandbags, the commanding officer, Colonel Hollis, was hit in the head. The next moment Fitshell thought he, too, had been hit but it turned out to be a piece of brick flung up by a shell which numbed his leg.

Still trying to reach Boulogne, Leonard Green and his companions from the RASC at Lille eventually found a Red Cross train on which they begged a lift. Since the Geneva Convention forbade guns in ambulances or on Red Cross trains, the medical officer in charge insisted that they throw away their rifles. It so upset Green he insisted on having the order in writing before he complied. He also made a point of getting rid of his identity card which stated his religion as Jewish.

Near St Omer, as the train halted, on the road running alongside the track they saw a convoy of tanks approaching which they assumed to be the French 70-tonners they had heard about. It was only as the monsters lurched forward, their turrets traversing, that they caught sight of an open staff car with an officer standing up in it, just as in the newsreels they had seen.

'Christ!' came the shout. 'They're not French! They're Jerries!'

Almost at the same moment a burst of machine-gun fire hit the train and as the order was given, 'Every man for himself', Green and his companions dived out of the far side into a wheatfield where the tall standing corn gave them cover.

Gunner Webb's battery, after its narrow escape near the Scarpe, had reached Seclin where they were greeted with the news that Calais and Boulogne had fallen. Swinging west, they found defensive lines being overrun again and again and moving, to Wytschaete, overlooking Ypres, the Flanders plain and World War I battlefields, they hid their guns and vehicles among the trees. The Cameron Highlanders were occupying a position covering the La Bassée Canal crossings from which they could see the Germans massing for an attack. Webb's gun was in the garden of a house with a ridge in front so that it was obscured from view, but they could see a German observation balloon hanging in the sky and they guessed they had been spotted.

By now signals reaching England were reporting a steady increase in shellfire from the Calais area and it became clear that the main approach route to Dunkirk was going to be too dangerous to use in daylight. The Isle of Man packet *Mona's Queen* had already been riddled with shrapnel from the shore, yet at 4 pm two hospital ships passed Calais, which lay under a heavy pall of smoke, and began to pick their way through the wrecks that already littered Dunkirk harbour. *Maid of Orleans*, with a cargo of 2 gallon cans of water and men who were to help with the port facilities, also arrived through the shelling to find the harbour under air attack and had to return to Dover. Trying again later, she berthed safely.

Dunkirk was already a shambles. To the west the oil tanks were blazing, flames from burning warehouses silhouetted the jetties, and throughout the night bombs continued to crash into the town. As the thud of these bombs reached Dover, Ramsay's staff began to think of lifting men from the open beaches. But there was a desperate shortage of small boats, and it was only then that an immense and readily available source was remembered.

On 14 May, through the BBC, the Admiralty had requested all owners of self-propelled pleasure craft between 30 and 100 feet in length to send in their particulars. It had had nothing to do with the possibility of an evacuation and was merely a step taken by the

Admiralty Small Vessels Pool because the German magnetic mine campaign had taken away most of the wooden vessels coming from the boatyards, and it had been decided that they could be replaced for harbour and auxiliary work by requisitioned private vessels.

Immediately, all officers who could be spared from the Pool were sent to yachting centres. *King Alfred,* the Royal Naval Volunteer Reserve (RNVR) training establishment, was signalled and other signals were sent to the Flag Officer, Port of London, the C-in-C, Plymouth, and other naval commands, while yachtsmen who had already sent in particulars of their boats as a result of the BBC broadcast were telephoned. The boats began to move.

By midnight this day, a total of 27,936 men had been brought home, mostly the men of the 'useless mouths' scheme.

MONDAY 27 MAY

At dawn on the 27th, just as civilian England was stirring, German panzers were rattling north once more in a vast pincer movement. Hitler had changed his mind and ordered his armour to advance again—but only to within 13 miles of Dunkirk. The idea was that the Kleist Group should drive east between Gravelines and Robecq, while in the south the Hoth Group should head towards Armentières and Kemmel to cut off the BEF, encircle the French First Army, pierce the rear of General Brooke's front, and link up with Bock's Sixth Army. After that it was up to Goring to finish the job, though General Albert Kesselring, of Luftflotte 2, whose units were already reduced to 50 per cent by casualties and wear and tear, was far from enthusiastic.

And unfortunately the gap was closed just twenty-four hours too late, and the BEF and a third of the French First Army slipped clear. Second Division, fighting without support against tremendous attacks, fell slowly back over the battlefields of 1914–18, making stands as they went from ditches, houses, and roadblocks of farmcarts and old bedsteads.

As the last of the British slipped through, with them was Dr Laurence de R. Epps, of the Royal Army Medical Corps (RAMC). In a flush of patriotism when he had qualified in 1937, he had tried to join the RNVR but, as there were no vacancies, he had opted for the Territorials, which also had to turn him down for the same reason. Joining the supplementary reserve, when war broke out he found himself with the 1st Field Ambulance of the 1st Guards Brigade but now, as they moved back through Roubaix, he was temporarily detached to the Cheshire Regiment. Near Poperinghe, however, without informing him what they were doing, the Cheshires split up into the fields and he was left with his driver alone in the road. An obvious movement was taking place to Dunkirk so he followed the stream of vehicles. Up to then he had not seen a shot fired and the only casualty he had treated was a man who had accidentally shot himself in the foot.

Poperinghe itself was chaotic, but the colonel of the 2nd Coldstream had enlisted a troop of Belgian Boy Scouts to guide his battalion through. Subaltern James Langley, who up to then had regarded the

Scout movement with derision, changed his attitude the moment he saw the Belgian boys waiting unmoved among the swirling mass of men, horses and guns that choked the debris-littered street.

One of the last men out of Belgium was Sir Brian Horrocks. He arrived in the dark on the Escaut Canal to find most of the bridges blown. Crossing the sole intact one, he was asked, 'Any more of our troops on the far side?' 'I can guarantee there are none,' Horrocks replied, and up went the bridge.

As at Mons in 1914, it was the high standard of training and the discipline and toughness of the regimental officers and men that helped the BEF to weather the storm. Nevertheless, the road back was a nightmare with the crowds of refugees and the despondent columns of French and Belgian soldiers with their inevitable horsedrawn transport. Always there were the rumours: the panzers were here, there, everywhere; parachutists were behind them; such and such a unit had been wiped out. Under the circumstances, morale should have sunk to zero but, oddly enough, it did not, and the men marched on towards the north-west curiously indifferent to the chaos around them. In the heat, they were often in their shirt sleeves and some of them had torn branches from trees for use as sticks so that there was a strange feeling of a 'vast summer hike' going on. And as with that other BEF in 1914, the soldiers' sense of humour was never far from evident. When asked by Horrocks how they were getting on, one company commander replied, 'Don't look round, sir. I think we're being followed.' The chief menace was not so much the Germans as exhaustion. The only man who seemed unaffected, Horrocks noticed, was Montgomery who always had his meals at the right time and a proper night's sleep, so that he arrived at Dunkirk as fresh as when he had started. 'He was about the only one who was,' Horrocks commented.

Food was becoming a tremendous problem. The thousands of men cramming into the dwindling area of space were beginning to find it difficult to feed themselves. Gunner Bain had a reputation for being able to find anything in the way of food, and now the commanding officer asked him if he could manage it once again. He milked cows, caught stray chickens, collected zinc baths full of eggs which he filled with water and boiled, and, on one occasion, chased a pig in his truck to provide the only meat they had had for some time.

It was the search for food which ended the freedom of Leonard Green and his companions from the Red Cross train. Hot, footsore and hungry, they were trying to find a farm where they might get a meal when a German tank appeared and started blazing away with its

machine-gun, wounding one of them. Finding an abandoned ambulance, they pushed the injured man in the back and started off for the
coast, only for it to dawn on them that they were behind, not in front
of, the German lines and that, instead of heading away from trouble,
they were heading into it. Almost immediately, they ran straight into
a German machine-gun nest that occupied both sides of the road. In
a moment there were grey-clad figures on all sides of them and the
Germans did not even bother to open fire.

Late on the night of the 26th, Gort had given the defence of Dunkirk to
Sir Ronald Adam of Third Corps. Admiral Abrial, the French *Amiral
Nord*, had been commanded to hold the same perimeter by Weygand
but had been given only two divisions under General Fagalde to do it
with. On the morning of the 27th, Adam and Fagalde met at Cassel
where the British and French areas of operation were decided. At
the conference it became clear from Weygand's representative that
Weygand was quite out of touch and was still thinking of an attack
towards the south-west and the recapture of Calais.

With Cassel besieged, headquarters were moved north and, as they
were being set up, Gort received yet another message from Eden,
informing him that his sole task was to evacuate to England as many
of his men as possible. Far from happy with the French reaction at
the Cassel conference, he headed for Dunkirk to contact Blanchard
and, while there, learned something which had been reported to his
headquarters after he had left by Admiral Sir Roger Keyes, at Belgian
HQ: the King of the Belgians had asked for an armistice, and his left
flank was open to the sea.

The fighting this day was terrific. Most of the German attacks fell
on the 2nd Division along the La Bassée Canal. With their positions
in ideal tank country, by noon the 6th Brigade had been overrun and
wiped out. The same fate came to the 4th Brigade, comprising the
2nd Norfolks, the 1st Royal Scots and the 8th Lancashire Fusiliers.
Junkers transports landed troops on the very edge of the British
positions and the Fusiliers were mopped up after a bitter fight. The
Norfolks, surrounded by tanks and infantry in farm buildings at Le
Paradis, decided to surrender, but as the acting commanding officer,
Major Ryder, appeared in the doorway with a white flag and a small
group of men, they were mown down by machine-guns. As the firing
ceased, fit and wounded—among them Major Ryder—were herded
into a field where, quite cold-bloodedly, they were murdered with
machine-guns, SS troops afterwards moving among the bodies to

finish off the survivors with revolvers and bayonets. Reduced to little more than a company, the Royal Scots were also lined up to be shot by the SS, but were saved by a senior officer of the Wehrmacht who happened to pass.

As the Germans pushed forward, from Wytschaete—the famous Messines Ridge of World War I—Gunner Webb watched the infantry in front constantly pounded. On one occasion when a stray bomb whistled down in their direction, one of his friends dived for shelter into one of the ancient pillboxes from World War I, only to find he had landed in the accumulated filth and slime of twenty years. Guns, rifles, Brens and mortars were going and soon afterwards they had the unnerving experience of seeing the Wiltshire Regiment coming back over the ridge and through their positions as Brigadier M. C. Dempsey, of 13th Brigade, decided to withdraw to higher ground. There were now no infantry at all in front of them.

Behind them the road stretched away from the village. On it was a bend with a barn that was perfectly pinpointed by German artillery. Trucks heading for it at full speed slapped on their brakes as the shells screamed down, then, as they exploded, accelerated at full speed again past the spot. Four trucks had been lost there and one old Wiltshire reservist, when asked where his transport was, announced, 'I'm fucking walking. You won't get me in a truck.'

Shortly afterwards they saw the Cameronians also moving back. They had been engaged in heavy fighting and while drawing back some of them overshot the position they were expecting to occupy and had to be brought forward again with the Wiltshires and other troops to throw the Germans back. As the counter-attack went in, Webb's battery, watched by a German Henschel spotter plane, was firing through open sights to knock out scouting machine-gun patrols. They were a Territorial unit and most of Webb's friends on the guns had been to the same school in the East End of London with him. They gave a sufficiently good account of themselves to draw a tribute from Lieutenant-Colonel G. D. Rose-Miller, of the Cameronians. 'Some distance in the rear,' he said, 'two troops of a field battery served their guns as well as they could under the direct observation of the Henschel. They kept firing and, though the drifting smoke . . . obscured their view, they harassed the German infantry and drove them . . . over the ridge.'

The position that morning at sea was equally confused and ships were being forced back by the guns at Calais and the attacks of the

Luftwaffe. Though *Mona's Isle* got away early from Dunkirk, she was soon spotted by the guns at Gravelines and shortly afterwards by prowling aircraft. As the bombs and machine-gun bullets raked her crowded decks, twenty-three men were killed and sixty wounded. MV *Sequacity* was hit by a shell which struck her port side and passed clean through her, then by one which struck her starboard side and smashed into her engine room, wrecking auxiliaries. A third shot struck the wheel-house and went downwards through the hold and out through the ship's bottom. *Yewdale,* a little tramp with a crew of only eleven, stood by her as she launched her lifeboat and, despite the bombing and shelling, picked up her crew as she went down by the head and disappeared.

It was becoming very clear that the 30-mile route to Dunkirk from Dover along the coast near Calais known as Route Z would have to be abandoned during daylight. There were two other possibilities: Route Y, 87 miles long, from Dover to the North Goodwin Light then east to the Kwinte Buuoy and back on its tracks to Dunkirk along the coast at Nieuport and La Panne through the Zuydecoote Pass; and Route X, 55 miles long, across the Ruytingen Bank to the inshore channel between Gravelines and Dunkirk. Route X was known to be mined. Route Y was thought to be possibly mined. Ramsay had to accept the risk and ships were ordered to proceed by Route Y.

That morning, despite the difficulties, Basil Bartlett finally reached Dunkirk. His section had passed through burning Armentières and, due to the jams on the roads, were constantly passed in their vehicles by marching infantry they had passed earlier. The journey had seemed to consist chiefly of jumping in and out of ditches. Dunkirk was a shock. He knew it had been bombed but had no idea how bad it was. The town mayor's office, crowded with officers and men seeking information, was bedlam. Everyone was asking for ships but nothing could get in and he was told to head for the harbour in case a ship made it during the night.

Returning to his section at Furnes, they destroyed their vehicles and threw away their spare clothes, which the local people and the Belgians promptly snatched up, the Belgians using their rifles to get the best. All along the road was an orgy of destruction under a brilliant blue sky. By the time he returned to Dunkirk with his men, the situation had already deteriorated. The town was blazing and there were huge columns of flame and smoke coming from the docks. All the air-raid shelters were full, and there was no water, light or food, and then an ammunition truck caught fire and started to blow up in all directions.

The fighting went on all day. At Watten, Colonel Strudwick's unit were ordered to put their huge guns out of action. They could not blow them up because of their size, so they smashed the sighting and elevation gear and pushed them into the canal, considering their weight alone would make them difficult to salvage.

By this time there was little left of the 2nd Royal Sussex. They had been surrounded and their escape almost cut off. The 7th Royal Sussex, separated from Brigade headquarters and from the 6th after the bombing of the trains at Amiens, became mixed with French regiments astride the road to Poix and Rouen, where they were overwhelmed. Their colonel captured, their second-in-command shot for not surrendering quickly enough, only 200 of them survived.

Many of the French villages were a-flutter with white already. 'From every house . . . from church steeples, farms, cottages . . . there flapped a white flag . . . a white table cloth, sheet, towel or handkerchief.' Here and there little knots of silent people stood by the wayside as BEF streamed back, but the majority were peering through closed shutters, waiting for the Germans to arrive. At Ypres there was a 5-mile-long traffic jam of refugee cars and Army vehicles, and when the air attacks began, a supply lorry was hit and two loaded ambulances went up in bright orange pyres. One of the drivers had been flattened by the blast against the metal of his cab and what remained of him was left hanging out of the open door.

In one such raid, Trooper Gillam managed to pick up 2,000 cigarettes and 2,000 razor blades from a burning NAAFI waggon. Men were already beginning to destroy what they could not carry, and he ended up like the others with nothing but a haversack, his equipment and a rifle.

As units became interlocked, the confusion increased. A French artillery regiment, near-missed by a bomb, scattered in confusion towards a British battery, shouting and yelling, 'the drivers . . . whipping up the horses . . . gunners clinging frantically to limbers, ammunition trailers, mess carts, GS waggons'.

They were now entering the coastal area of low-lying fields. These stretched as far as the eye could see and into this pancake of land it seemed as if the whole of the BEF was pouring. Every road was a thick mass of transport and troops, great long lines stretching back to the horizon, all converging on Dunkirk, all crawling over the featureless country in the late sunshine. Under their camouflage paint they looked like 'slow-moving rivers of muddy-coloured lava from some far-off eruption'.

At this point, regiments started the doleful process of wrecking their equipment. New wireless sets were placed in rows while a soldier with a pick-axe knocked them to pieces. Truck radiators and engines were smashed with sledgehammers, tyres were slashed and sawn. The canals became choked with wrecks all piled one on top of another until 'there was more wreck than water'.

On the struggling men the Germans were dropping leaflets as well as bombs. 'You are surrounded,' they said in English. 'The match is ended. Throw down your arms. We take prisoners.' The approach to the French was different, and accused the country's leaders of leaving the troops in the lurch.

Gunner Eric Clark, of the signals section of the 98th Field Regiment, a friend of Gunner Hammond, the tractor driver, had a specialist duty working in a truck with an officer, signaller and driver. His job was to observe where the enemy were, work out the position on the map and hand it to the radio operator who sent it to the guns. Having done a long stint at the job, his place was taken that evening by another man who went off with Captain Lord Cowdray, a popular officer who, when the Army had been unable to provide boots for the unit, had gone out with a truck and bought them a load of French ones. Clark was lucky. The truck ran into an ambush; a burst of machine-gun fire almost cut the driver in two, killed the man who had taken Clark's place, wounded the radioman and shattered Cowdray's arm. Despite his dreadful wound, Cowdray somehow managed to drive the lorry several miles back to safety.

Brought back during the previous night to the Ypres-Comines Canal, the 3rd Grenadier Guards, who had lost 180 men in their last action, were sent into the attack again with the North Staffordshires. Guardsman Eldridge had just marched 20 miles back under very trying conditions but on arrival they were ordered to help restore the front of the 50th Division. Without food, they now had to march 9 miles to the start line and from there another 3 miles over unknown country to attack an enemy whose strength and positions were also unknown.

The two regiments advanced separately. The North Staffords reached to within a mile of the canal. The Grenadiers, with the Black Watch—by now reduced to three weak companies—and a Field Company of the Royal Engineers somewhere on their right, advanced against mounting opposition in the increasing darkness until only two officers were left, finally going in with the bayonet to put to flight the Germans in front of the canal.

Gort had committed his last reserves and it was now up to the unknown men fighting for villages and bridges and crossroads and stretches of Belgian waterways. It was no longer possible to hold on to the Lys and, as the Belgian Army crumbled, it was time to set up the last perimeter and man it.

Sir Brian Horrocks was at 3rd Division HQ when Brooke called to see Montgomery. Brooke had a habit of speaking in short clipped sentences, always the brisk warrior, but according to Horrocks, he was a consummate actor. Very much a family man and a keen bird-watcher, he hated war yet at no time except one, of which Horrocks was later to be a witness, did he give the slightest indication of the emotions he must have felt. The situation he disclosed could hardly have been worse. The 5th Division, commanded by General Franklyn, was being heavily attacked and had not yet established contact with the 50th Division on its left. If the 5th gave way, then the whole front would crumble, and Brooke proposed to reinforce it with everything he could lay his hands on.

There was worse to come. On the extreme left, the Belgians had already ceased to exist as a fighting force and had left a wide gap into which the Germans were likely to pour at any moment. To fill the gap, Montgomery's 3rd Division was ordered to carry out one of the most difficult manoeuvres in war—withdraw from the line and move to the north, along small roads only a few thousand yards in the rear of the embattled 5th Division which might well break at any moment. It would have been difficult at any time but with the congestion on the roads, it looked well nigh impossible. Yet Montogmery took it in his stride. His orders were clear and concise and he seemed completely confident, even cocky, convinced he was the best divisional commander in the army. By the time he reached Dunkirk, Horrocks agreed with him.

'Of course the Third Division will get there,' he said. And they did. The vehicles moved at times under an arc of fire from the batteries covering the battle. Behind them the 4th and 42nd Divisions fell back and the 1st Division passed through them. It was nowhere neat and there were long unmanned sectors, but slowly the lines took shape and a new front was established.

When the news came at midnight that the Belgians had surrendered, Horrocks noticed a Belgian soldier working with a party of British Engineers. He 'looked as if he had been pole-axed', and with a stricken look on his face, he put on his equipment saluted and walked away towards the Germans. 'Je ne suis pas lache, moi—comme les autres,' he said. 'I'm not a coward like the others'. His solitary figure disappearing towards the enemy seemed to Horrocks to accentuate the shame of his country's defeat.

The new route from Dover to Dunkirk, though clear of the fire from shore batteries, doubled the sailing time and increased the chances for the Luftwaffe, but Fighter Command of the RAF ordered patrols over the area from 5 am until dusk.

Though they were not often seen, the RAF were desperately trying to hold off the Germans. Flight Lieutenant Stanford Tuck had just shot down an ME 110 and had seen the pilot scramble clear. With no hard feelings, he circled low to wave and as the German raised his arm Tuck thought he was waving back. Instead a bullet clipped through the windscreen's side panel to within six inches of his face and he realised the German was holding an automatic pistol. Turning away, he came back deliberately and fired so that the German pitched on his face and lay with the smoke of his burning plane drifting over him.

Wing Commander Basil Embry also took off as the day drew to a close. His job was to attack the German columns pursuing the BEF. He had been flying continuously since the beginning of the war and under heavy pressure since 10 May. On 12 May he had led a wing of Blenheims in a second attempt from England on the Maastricht bridges and of the twenty-four aircraft he led, seven were left burning on the ground and two more crash-landed on return, while all the rest were hit in some way. He had also joined the 14 May attack on the German bridgehead at Sedan, losing 25 per cent of his force, so that his squadron no longer possessed a single serviceable aircraft. By 20 May, however, they had been refitted and were at it again. On 26 May he was informed he had been appointed to command an RAF station with the rank of group captain. He resented being taken off flying, but he knew he was tired because one morning he had fallen asleep while dressing and on another occasion while drinking a glass of beer. On fifteen occasions since 11 May he had brought home a damaged aeroplane. Now, he was to have just one more go.

They dropped their bombs, but just as Embry started to turn, his window was blown open, he felt a jab of pain in his left leg and the control column was almost wrenched from his grasp. The rear gunner was dead and, as the two surviving crew members crouched near the tiny escape hatch with the aeroplane spiralling down, Embry put his foot in the back of his observer and pushed him through. A moment or two later, he struggled clear himself, to parachute down behind the German lines near St Omer. Far from defeated, when confronted by a German captain who told him to salute, he retorted smartly that he was equivalent to a colonel. 'In the British services,' he snapped, 'it's the usual custom for a captain to salute first.' He was taken before a general he later identified as Guderian, whom he thought looked more British than German. Since he was shivering with cold, Guderian handed him a coat so that he was driven off to captivity dressed, he said, as a German general.

Despite the efforts being made by the RAF, the numbers were nevertheless small and the patrols made little impact. As Adolf Galland said, 'We saw little of the RAF', and Dunkirk continued to be bombed.

The previous day Captain W. G. Tennant, who had just been appointed captain of the battle cruiser *Repulse*, had volunteered to help. Ordered to Dunkirk as Senior Naval Officer ashore, on this Monday, with a staff of 12 officers, 160 ratings and a communications group, he arrived in HMS *Wolfhound*. Most of the harbour facilities had been wrecked and the town had descended into chaos. The roadside was littered with blazing wrecks and 2 million gallons of oil were going up in a huge black column that coiled into the upper air where it hung in a flat pall over the coast. The streets were full of rubble and burning vehicles, and dazed French and Belgian soldiers were standing in shocked groups. Hundreds more had collected at the station but they were now directed to the beach where the slow process of lifting by ships' boats had been going on for some time.

The cellars of the town were full of the flotsam of the retreat, mostly French but with a fair sprinkling of British, most of them lines of communication troops who had been less retreating soldiers than refugees, some stragglers, a few deserters, and a few who had genuinely lost touch with their units. Many were drunk and beginning to roam the town and Captain Tennant himself disarmed the leader of one such gang and persuaded the men to join a queue.

There was clearly a desperate need for action, and he signalled 'Please send every available craft to beaches east of Dunkirk immediately. Evacuation tomorrow is problematical.' When to his signal was added a report from the BEF that the situation was precarious, Ramsay ordered all available ships across. Patrolling destroyers were called in and the anti-aircraft cruiser *Calcutta*, destroyers, transports, minesweepers, drifters and skoots began to work the beaches with their boats.

Cross-Channel steamers also began to arrive. Late in the evening *Queen of the Channel*, a fast motor ship which had been employed for some months as a leave ship between England and France, had just entered the harbour and picked up fifty men when she was ordered out to lie off the beaches and put down lifeboats to pick up the men waiting there. In fact, these deep-sea lifeboats were far from suitable for shallow-water work and, with the loading painfully slow, Tennant now decided to experiment with the East Mole. It was long and narrow and had never been intended for ships, but it offered the hope of quick embarkation.

With *Queen of the Channel* handy, he ordered her to go alongside. Moving at dead slow speed, her captain nudged her into position through the darkness until she finally bumped gently against the wooden piles. The mole was long enough to accommodate many ships at once and for the first time it seemed there was a glimmer of hope. *Queen of the Channel* had taken 600 men on board and cut her mooring ropes when more men were heard running towards her. She nosed in again for them to clamber aboard and the captain went stern-first out of the harbour under continuous air raids to pick up his boats.

Although the French government had been informed what was happening, nothing was passed on to their Navy, but one or two men of energy began to improvise, and all available naval craft were ordered up. In England, the Small Vessels Pool had set up a headquarters at Sheerness and boat builders were asked to act as agents. With a complete absence of red tape, the boats began to move.

The day ended with little success, however. Only 7,669 men had been landed in England. But, although it was not yet realised, Tennant's decision to use the East Mole was to prove the turning point of the whole operation and the salvation of the BEF.

TUESDAY 28 MAY

As 28 May opened, Churchill warned the House of Commons of 'hard and heavy tidings'. He did not, however, ever contemplate treating with Hitler. Neither did anyone else, either in England or on the beaches of Dunkirk.

As he was speaking, the last of the divisions fighting in the east slipped into their places and the flank now came under Brooke's command. The German movement had been a gigantic right wheel on Ypres and, though it was executed with parade ground precision, it was just not fast enough, and the leading elements were met by the ubiquitous 12th Lancers.

Colonel Lumsden had suspected for some time that the Belgians would no longer be able to defend the vital bridges over the Yser at Dixmude and Nieuport, and had sent off a troop to one and a weak squadron to the other with orders to blow them up. The patrol at Dixmude under Second Lieutenant E. C. Mann, saw a black Mercedes, carrying a white flag and containing four heavily armed Germans, race out of the town to the bridge where one of the Germans was seen in conversation with French and Belgian officers. As the car returned to Dixmude, a French major informed the Lancers that he was taking over the defence of the bridge and that the British should withdraw. Mann ignored the order and was now joined by Lieutenant D. A. Smith, of the Engineers. The bridge had already been prepared for demolition and the Belgians were forced at revolver point to explain how the charge worked. Just as Smith set it off, a host of German motor cyclists arrived on the other side, to be met by a torrent of fire from the Lancers. They were followed by dozens of lorries loaded with troops but Mann and his men stopped all attempts to cross, while the German onslaught against Nieuport was blocked by the heroic defence of a mixed force of British and the French 60th Division.

On the opposite side of the pocket, British strongpoints fell one after the other, and the battle was conducted by generals and brigadiers without contact with headquarters. By late in the morning, the leading tanks were a bare 8 miles from Dunkirk and the moles were coming under fire. But the ditches, the raised roads, and the flooded fields now stopped the tanks dead once more and Guderian decided against further attacks.

In fact, there was little to oppose him and he could have carried Bergues and pushed into Dunkirk, but the decision he made allowed the BEF to slip away, though six divisions of the French First Army, chiefly due to the confusion at French headquarters, were cut off. General Prioux claimed his men were too tired to withdraw further, and General Blanchard decided that evacuation from the open beaches was impossible anyway. While they vacillated, other French generals showed courage and decision. Two divisions under General Molinié continued to fight on at Haubourdin, and General de la Laurencie brought out the French Third Corps and the cavalry. Laurencie had received orders that his regiments were to burn their colours. 'Why this act of despair?' he snapped. 'We are not yet on our knees . . . My men can and *will* fight.'

By now, Adams' measures for the defence of the perimeter were in effect and Tennant's decision to use the East Mole was already beginning to pay dividends. During the night he had set up a control system, arranged berthing parties, and appointed Commander J. C. Clouston as piermaster. Destroyers went in, loaded and, pulling out stern-first headed for Dover. Personnel ships were quickly ordered in to back them up.

It was about this time that Lieutenant-Colonel G. C. Viner became beachmaster at La Panne, taking his instructions from Lord Gort himself at GHQ, which had finally been established in a chateau there. La Panne had been an artists' colony, with hotels, trees, parks and gardens, but now bodies were being collected by air-raid wardens and lorries and cars were burning in the streets.

Viner was in the RAOC but had served ten years in the Royal Marines. En route to the coast, he had spotted an excellent pair of long German field-glasses lying by the side of the road and when he arrived he was wearing them around his neck. On the beach was a Bofors gun commanded by a subaltern who was trying to watch approaching Stukas with a pair of opera glasses and Viner offered the big binoculars in their place.

The subaltern was overwhelmed. 'What can we do for you in return?' he asked.

Dusty and tired, Viner said half-jokingly, 'You can provide me with a bath.'

He got one. Water was heated and he took it on the beach in an officer's canvas bath. What was more, he got one every day after that, in full view of everybody. It had an extraordinary effect on morale, he said—not only his own but everybody else's too.

There was little organisation when he arrived, with neither ships nor boats arriving, but he discovered that the undersea cable had not yet been cut, and the first thing he did was ring Dover and get in touch with Ramsay's headquarters to demand ships.

'You've got them,' he was told.

Viner exploded, 'You'd better come and look for yourself,' he said.

By afternoon, the situation had improved. Tows of whalers and ships' lifeboats began to arrive, not only at La Panne but also at Bray Dunes and Malo-les-Bains, and minesweepers were coming from all round Britain. The paddle minesweepers working the new channels were also sent in as personnel carriers, and destroyers moved from the North Sea and the east coast to join the Dover flotilla, while tugs, yard craft and coasters also headed across. They were all manned by professional seamen, though there were a few amateurs who had insisted on getting in on the act.

Dover harbour was already packed with ships and more were anchored in the Downs among the wrecks of the magnetic mine campaign. At night they carried no lights and those buoys which had not been removed or sunk were also unlit. Yet, despite the efforts of the Navy to provide them, ships' masters often had to pick they way through without charts. One convoy of three all grounded in the Zuydecoote Pass, one remaining fast for several hours.

As they went out, others returned, often smaller vessels such as drifters and fishing boats, carrying men who had marched for days across France, dirty, dishevelled, their eyes bloodshot with weariness. Near the Kwinte buoy one boat had picked up survivors, some of them women, from a small French vessel which had struck a mine. Their clothes had been ripped off by the explosion and almost every one of them was suffering from fractures of the legs, pelvis or spine.

They had to push their way through the southward stream of whooping destroyers, Deal beach craft, boats with registrations from the Wash to Poole, mud hoppers, coal barges, yachts, trawlers smelling of fish, Dutch skoots stinking of onions and still decorated with geraniums, their crews professional sailors, old soldiers, men from the Scottish islands, a few brave Americans and more than one nobleman. They were all supposed to have signed a form which made them naval men for a month to cover their families in case of death, but many of them had not got around to it. Some managed to stow a few rations on board; some did not. Some wore helmets they had picked up; some wore helmets from World War I; some had only metal balers and enamel bowls to hold over their heads. Some had charts; some were told simply to head for the sound of the guns. 'The need to get trained men back to train others is paramount' were their orders.

As they crowded the narrow approach to Dunkirk, the air raids came again and collisions occurred as ships travelling at full speed tried in the narrow confines to take evading action. The number of wrecks littering the fairway increased. The dock area was also full of wreckage—a burning train, cranes canted out of true, ambulances punctured with bullets and shell splinters. Bodies lay about among the scattered brickwork, covered with greatcoats, gas capes or ground sheets, their heavy boots sticking up in ungainly fashion.

Although ships could load quickly against the jetties, off the beaches they had to wait for hours as the small boats laboriously brought out men from the shore. One of them, the personnel carrier *Abukir,* was attacked by an E-boat near the North Hinder Buoy, and *Queen of the Channel,* which had done so well the previous day, was bombed by a solitary aircraft. Her back broken, she was sinking fast when *Dorrian Rose,* an elderly tramp which had been used as a store ship, came alongside and transferred everybody from the dying vessel in a matter of thirty-five minutes. With 1,000 men on board, she headed for Dover.

Though the French were still not officially participating in the evacuation, it had been decided to bring out 'specialists' and the first French ships had just cleared the entrance of the harbour when *Douaisien* was sunk by a magnetic mine.

Most of the work was being done by destroyers, their crews packing the soldiers into every inch of space not occupied by engines, guns or torpedo tubes. As they embarked more and more, they became top-heavy, and heeled over at incredible angles as they took evading actions against the bombs. But the soldiers were now being lifted at tremendous speed and colossal risks were being taken, the destroyer captains slamming their ships against the pier or between the bigger cross-Channel ferries as if they had been built to do the same work.

Everybody, naval and civilian seamen alike, accepted the dangers, and some were unlucky. The destroyers *Wolsey* and *Windsor* were both damaged; *Pangbourne,* a coal-burning paddle minesweeper, ran aground but managed to claw off; and *Brighton Belle,* the oldest paddle minesweeper afloat, ripped her bottom out on the wreck of a ship sunk a few hours earlier. There were so many ships about, however, all her troops and crew—even the captain's dog—were rescued.

With the vast number of ships now appearing, the Army gained heart and began to organise itself.

Captain Bartlett had spent a cheerless night on the beach and as more men arrived he was put in command of his own small area of sand. The men around him were all strangers, but they were patient and sensible and allowed themselves to be divided into groups of twenty-five and tucked away in the dunes until their turn came. The day was hot and the Germans never left them alone. But scattered men dug into the sand did not make good targets and casualties were light. Whenever an aeroplane was shot down into the sea there were wild cheers. There was a strange Bank Holiday atmosphere, in fact, but gunfire always sent everyone running for the trenches in the dunes. At 4 pm the Navy returned and with them the Luftwaffe, in waves. Discipline was tremendous, however, and except for those actually embarking, everyone kept off the beach. Naval AA guns were going intermittently all day and they saw no RAF fighters but, since the German attacks slackened, they could only assume they were at work somewhere out of sight.

The RAF were there all right but, curiously, many of them knew remarkably little about what was going on. The Army had laid such a screen of secrecy over the evacuation, most of the airmen had no idea that the beaches were filling with exhausted men, least of all people like the legless pilot, Douglas Bader, with 222 Squadron, who had been flying from near Grimsby well to the north. Moving to Felixstowe, the squadron took off for the French coast and, as they approached Dunkirk, he saw a strange black plume floating hugely over the sea. A voice over the radio said 'That looks like it. That's smoke. Must be burning oil tanks', and for a long time they circled at 12,000 feet. Their orders were to go no lower and they left without seeing any German aircraft at all. Yet beneath them the Stukas and Messerschmitts were staining the sand with blood, and British fighters from other squadrons were low down over the beaches.

Among them was Flying Officer Alan Deere. His squadron, 54, had been continuously in action and by the previous day had been reduced to eight aircraft and twelve very tired pilots, and it was into the black pall of smoke over Dunkirk which Bader saw that one of his friends had disappeared on the tail of a Stuka, never to be seen again. By this time the surviving pilots were literally on their last legs and it came as a relief to learn they were being withdrawn the next day and were to do their last patrol at dawn.

The captured Wing Commander Embry, meanwhile, after one unsuccessful attempt to escape, had been lodged in a church at

Hucqueliers. The confusion seemed as bad on the German side as it was on the British, and he decided that if he were ever to escape this was the time.

Lance-Corporal Mays, trying by this time to get to Dunkirk with his radio van, had run into hordes of refugees who had been bombed and machine-gunned and he was kneeling by the side of a dying nun. She had been carrying a small child whose mother had been killed, and her feet were torn to shreds. As she lay in a pool of blood, Mays bandaged them and fed her water and small pieces of army biscuit. Before she died, she gave him a St Christopher medallion to keep him safe.

On the beaches desultory bombing and machine-gunning went on all day. In Dunkirk itself, there were tangled wires and dead horses everywhere, while blazing buildings made it impossible to move except on foot. As darkness came, the Germans put up flares which lit up the sky with a hard white light and aircraft constantly droned overhead. The glow from the flames could be seen for miles.

The sea was like glass, however, and to Captain Basil Bartlett it was tremendously exciting to hear the voices of the sailors and the splash of their oars. Again and again they came, and the comradeship on the beach was extraordinary, everybody sharing water bottles and biscuits without ever really seeing each other's faces.

The Germans had the range perfectly and were shelling the docks, yet the ships continued to take troops off the mole throughout the night. The mass of men in the town or still marching in was horrifying but everyone had a blind faith in the Navy and always remained highly optimistic of being saved. Among them was Private Cornford, the officers' mess cook, and his driver, who had been stopped and ordered to leave their vehicle.

'That way to Dunkirk,' they were told by a pointing military policeman, but Cornford had no idea why they were going there. All the roads were blocked by abandoned vehicles, but they squeezed through, tapping the radiators for water, because they had had none for days.

As the perimeter formed Bombardier Harold Sills, of 236 Battery, 59th Medium Regiment, RA, was serving 6in howitzers made in 1917. Arriving at Ghyvelde, they had been placed west of the canal there, with their sister battery, 235, on the east, only a footbridge connecting the two. There were many abandoned French cavalry horses in the neighbourhood and to keep their spirits up some of the men caught them and rode them round the field.

Guardsman Eldridge, still moving back, noticed how shrunken his battalion had become. They had suffered very heavy casualties, and now, exhausted and hungry, they were dispirited by the news of the Belgian surrender. The French seemed lackadaisical, with 'no initiative, and not much leadership or guts', and once he was shocked to see a crowd of British stragglers ambling back, whom he decided must be shell-shocked because they shuffled past with their heads down, their expressions gloomy.

Ordered to ditch their guns after their fine stand at Hazebrouck, the 98th Field Regiment threw away the firing pins and started to walk. Eighteen-year-old Gunner Hammond, hungry and already dog tired and half asleep, felt weariness like a weight on his head. They were all the same, their eyes closing, and weaving about the road as they marched. Fortunately, they were not troubled by aircraft and, as a small truck passed with the driver shouting 'Room for three', Hammond, already becoming an old soldier, scrambled aboard. In the back was a drunken Scottish sergeant waving a revolver and Hammond decided there was little wonder he was in the back alone.

Reaching the outskirts of Dunkirk, he saw his first dead bodies at close quarters. They were lying everywhere and he had to pick his way through them. On the beach was a regimental sergeant-major of the Guards who directed everybody with clarity and precision, brisk, upright and quite indifferent to the bombing and machine-gunning.

Not everybody was so lucky. Trying to take a wounded sergeant-major away from his unit in his Bren carrier, Lloyd George Fitsell found himself approaching a fork in the road. It crossed his mind that he ought not to take what appeared to be the main road, but as he was about to turn on to the minor road, he heard the order, 'Drive on'. Almost at once, like Lord Cowdray, they ran into an ambush. Armour-piercing bullets struck the front of the carrier and the sergeant sitting alongside him was hit in the chest. As a track was shot off, the carrier swerved into the ditch. Everybody had been hit except Fitsell and as he staggered from the wrecked vehicle he saw four Germans approaching him with a machine-gun.

Ambushes were common coin by this time and that evening, with Lord Cowdray wounded, Gunner Clark went out on the specialist duty with Lieutenant the Hon Bobby Blades. While crossing a field they were fired on and had to bolt at full speed, 'with smoke pouring from the engine and pieces flying off the vehicle in all directions'.

Ordered to man the perimeter, Gunner Webb's unit could not see the beaches but they could see the smoke, the aircraft and the parachutes of aircrew who had baled out. As dusk came, there was an incredible sense of desolation. In the houses around were a lot of refugees and on one occasion he saw a grandmother and her grandson clinging to each other in despair in their garden.

Sergeant Gough, who had continued to blow bridges all the way to the perimeter, was told to pick up more explosives, pass them out to artillerymen and show them how to destroy their guns. He and his section parked their vehicles in a big beetfield with thousands of others. More were arriving all the time and there was a steady crunching, chopping sound as cylinders and tanks were smashed. Four young conscripts had dug themselves a slit trench but when the Germans got the range, a shell landed in it and blew them clean out. They ran for twenty or thirty yards, dead men already with their insides spilling out.

When the artillerymen's turn to approach the beach came, Gough was sent to blow a bridge in the town. The place was being heavily shelled and naval missiles were whistling overhead to destroy vehicle parks, and there seemed to be only French soldiers about him, all without arms and equipment. The remnants of a dark-skinned French Moroccan Division were wearing their boots slung round their necks, and, although they had rifles, they had no ammunition and were terrified. The atmosphere about him was one of defeat and he came to the conclusion that the war was lost and the Allies were about to surrender. Then, as he returned, he saw a battalion of the Middlesex Regiment coming in from the rearguard. *They* were certainly not defeated, just exhausted, and when they halted, they simply flopped to the ground, with one exception—a soldier who was out of his mind and carried his webbing and rifle across his arms like a tray. He remained standing in that manner while all his friends fell asleep.

Colonel Strudwick had also reached Dunkirk now. At Watten, he had split his men into three or four groups to make the journey easier. They soon lost touch with each other but they all reached England, including fifty who were on board a ship which received a direct hit. They saw houses smashed by the bombing and at one point watches lying all over the pavement from a ruined jewellers.' A battery office was set up in a wine store, but, although no one had had any sleep or anything to drink for days, the drink was left untouched.

In their eagerness to get aboard the ships, the queues of soldiers lining up on the beaches began to edge into the water. At first they stood in the shallows but gradually they moved further and further out until they stood chest-high in the sea. A colossal improvisation was going on, but off the beaches the loading was still taking a long time as each destroyer had no more than two boats which could carry only twelve men at a time. Bartlett finally got aboard the destroyer *Grafton* and a Maltese steward handed him a sausage sandwich and a whisky. As he took off his shoes, socks and trousers and handed them to a steward to be dried he began to feel human again. It was an incredible contentment he felt. The Navy was in charge.

The feeling was beginning to run through the whole operation, in fact, that at last they were succeeding. In the twenty-four hours of this day, 17,804 men were brought back to safety. It seemed the answer had been found at last.

Major-General B. L. Montgomery—'not a popular figure'

Major-General Erwin Rommel, who smashed the French defences

Churchill and Vice-Admiral Bertram Ramsay inspecting charts

General Gerd von Runstedt

'... often they pushed their belongings in wheelbarrows, prams, even children's trolleys.' French refugees on the road

General Sir John Dill inspecting anti-tank preparations in a beet field

Camouflaged artillery in action

It soon became up to the individual British soldier

The blazing oil tanks of the Dunkirk, bombed by the Luftwaffe

Dunkirk harbour and dock basins

The soldiers were now being lifted at tremendous speed

Ramsay had barely a flotilla of destroyers, one of which is seen leaving Dunkirk

Opposite, top They were packed into any space not occupied by engines, guns or Torpedo tubes

Opposite, bottom Bodies were scattered everywhere. British dead on the sea front

Dazed French soldiers watch British troops march into Dunkirk

Fifteen thousand French soldiers had arrived in England by the end of May

Opposite, top 'Still the ships came.' British troops take their last look at Dunkirk

Opposite, bottom The gallant *Royal Daffodil*. One of the first ships at Dunkirk, she was finally disabled right at the end

'The whole of Dunkirk was a high wall of fire, the smoke pouring up in thick coils to the sky'

In their eagerness the men began to edge into the water

Soon only head and shoulders were above the sea and the dead weight of waterlogged boots and clothes pinned them down

As German aircraft appeared there was a fusillade of fire from the troops still on the beach

It was clear it was almost over now. A Lockheed Hudson approaching burning Dunkirk

Still they came ... stumbling ashore, wounded or exhausted

Finally silence, bodies in the sand, and wrecked vehicles

British and French prisoners, the sacrificed rearguard

WEDNESDAY 29 MAY

In the last hours of darkness that began 29 May, the two fronts of the BEF became a continuous line, with the 5th Division, under Franklyn, taking the heaviest pounding.

The division's positions were sited for the most part on forward slopes in full view of the Germans, and the canal which formed the front was not in use and completely dry. However, Brooke had managed to secure First Corps' artillery which was given to Franklyn with two other regiments of field guns and, though it was a long front, it was not impossible to hold it. In the west, the line also continued to hold, though the battle was still being fought by scratch units, often by non-combatant branches with limited weapons, insufficient ammunition and non-existent supplies. The garrison of Cassel, once Gort's headquarters, was now deep in enemy-held territory but continued to fight on stubbornly. Among them was Corporal George Wernham, of the 4th Oxford and Buckinghamshire Light Infantry, who had reached a ridge outside the town and dug in. As they waited, peering over their defences, Wernham could see the enemy tanks sweeping round both flanks and wondered what the next few days held for them.

At sea, even before daylight arrived, one of the most tragic incidents of the whole evacuation occurred. The destroyers *Wakeful* and *Grafton*, crammed with troops, were heading home by Route Y when *Wakeful* was torpedoed amidships. She had already done two trips and had a hole in her side from a near-miss from a bomb and now, as she was struck by the second of two torpedoes, the old destroyer broke in two and sank in a matter of seconds, carrying with her most of the 640 troops and crew she had on board. Most of them had been crammed below decks and they did not stand a chance.

The drifter *Nautilus* and the dan-layer *Comfort* began picking up the handful of survivors, among them the captain, Commander R. L. Fisher, and they were joined soon afterwards by *Grafton* and the minesweeper *Lydd*. As he was picked up, Fisher shouted a warning that the attacker was still at hand and as he did so a second salvo of torpedoes struck *Grafton*, lying motionless on the dark water among the wreckage from *Wakeful*. Her rails were crowded with troops, many of whom were killed instantly as the torpedoes tore into the destroyer's side.

The explosion blew Fisher into the water a second time from the deck of *Comfort*, and *Lydd* and *Grafton*, assuming that the low-lying shape of the drifter was an E-boat, opened fire on her. Men just rescued from the water were cut down by machine-guns and *Lydd*, sweeping round to the attack, rammed her steel bow into the drifter's wooden hull. As she went down, with her went most of her crew and all but four of *Wakeful's* survivors. Fisher, more dead than alive, was picked up by a Norwegian tramp steamer.

As *Grafton* had been hit, Bartlett, clad in battledress blouse and pyjama trousers, had been sleeping in the captain's cabin. As the torpedoes exploded he was flung unconscious to the deck and found himself stumbling about in the dark. There was strong smell of petrol and someone shouted 'For God's sake, don't light a match!' Struggling over the mounds of kit belonging to men who had been sleeping in the passageway, he found himself drenched by fuel oil and water pouring down from somewhere above his head. Reaching the deck, he was told to keep his head down as they were being machine-gunned and he saw what he took to be two German E-boats being fired at with tracer. Watching them sink, he crept out again, realising for the first time that when the torpedoes had flung him from his bunk, he had broken four of his front teeth. The ship was finished. The captain was dead in the wreckage of his bridge and the deck was a mass of twisted steel and mangled bodies which swearing, panting sailors were trying to heave out of the way.

One of the torpedoes had torn off the ship's stern and the second had exploded just beneath the wardroom where thirty-five officers, survivors from the beaches, were killed. But the wounded were brought out and as the ship began to list, everybody moved to the other side to counteract it. Then, as another ship arrived alongside at dawn, they transferred to that. There was perfect discipline and the men allowed themselves to be divided into groups with the same patience they had shown on the beaches, not one man moving out of turn.

Meanwhile, another destroyer, *Montrose*, returning with a full load of troops, had also been hit and lay within range of the Gris Nez searchlights, quite helpless, her bows blown away, until she was finally taken under tow stern-first. Three destroyers had been put out of action within an hour of the new day starting.

In England, first light came cold and wet as Alan Deere took off with 54 Squadron for their last trip. Crossing the coast near Gravelines, they were soon in action and Deere shot down a Dornier 17. But, as he did so, his own Spitfire was hit in the engine. He managed to ditch at the water's edge, just inside the perimeter and, with blood pouring down his face from a gash over his left eye, scrambled clear just as the Spitfire burst into flames.

At roughly the same time, Wing Commander Embry was marching rearwards in a column of prisoners. The guards were all riding in lorries and motor cycles, so he was careful to get a position on the opposite side of the column near the ditch. The confusion seemed as great as ever and as he passed a signpost marked 'Embry—3km', he decided it was an omen. Reaching a wooded area, he dived for the ditch and lay motionless as the column marched on without him, finally escaping through Spain to arrive in England in time to be involved in the Battle of Britain.

With daylight, the Luftwaffe appeared and the air raids began at once. Ships were heavily attacked but, despite the bombing, the work went on. But now another complication arose. Guns from Nieuport were brought to bear on Route Y where it turned close to the coast and the transport *Scotia* was the first ship to be hit. As the sea approaches shrank, Ramsay was forced to use the new central route and just before noon he sent the destroyers, *Jaguar*, *Gallant* and *Grenade* to check it. All three were bombed and *Gallant* damaged, but there was no firing from shore guns and by afternoon ships were being ordered to use the route, 'exercising navigational caution'. Considering the shells, bombs and torpedoes, navigational caution was the least of their worries.

Fed by smaller vessels, the cruiser *Calcutta* picked up 1,200 men from the beaches, and the coaster *Yewdale* over 1,000. The coaster *Bullfinch* was beached and troops climbed aboard her ladders. When she finally floated off on the rising tide, she had 1,500 men on board. *Royal Sovereign* also took home a full load, and by 5.30 pm was back off La Panne. The Isle of Man packet *Mona's Queen* was not so lucky. Just off Dunkirk she struck a mine and sank within two minutes. Released from his traffic duties at Ploegsteert and now on the beach, Lance-Corporal Warner could not believe a ship could disappear so fast.

The personnel ship *Killarney* passed her as she sank, to pick up 800 men and 'what appeared to be the whole canine population of France'. On the return journey, she was hit by a shell but still managed to pick up a French officer and two Belgian soldiers from a fragile raft made from an old door. They had stocked up well and had with them two tins of biscuits, six demijohns of wine and an ancient bicycle.

As *Killarney* left, her place was taken by the Southern Railways' vessel *Lochgarry*. As she cleared the harbour she had to wait for her escort, the destroyer *Greyhound*, but as *Greyhound* closed her, a shell hit her in the engine room. The Polish destroyer *Blyskawica* took her in tow.

While this was going on, Able Seaman Robert Hector, who had been only a week or so from his pension when the war had broken out, was on his way—although he did not yet know it—to Dunkirk. He had had his ship sunk under him off Norway and had been sent on fourteen days survivors' leave. He had had only eight of them when, to his disgust, he was summoned to return. On reaching his barracks, he was pushed with other men into a coach. They had no idea where they were going.

Meanwhile, on the other side of the Channel, his eye dressed by a Belgian girl, pilot Alan Deere was about to make for Ostend when he heard it had been captured and that the Belgian Army had surrendered. Boarding a civilian bus, therefore, he headed west, stole a bicycle from outside a shop and finally reached the outskirts of Dunkirk in an Army truck. The streets were choked with debris, dangling telephone wires and abandoned transport, while the smoke from the burning oil tanks hung over the town like a 'sentinel of death'. Among the troops waiting by the water's edge, one soldier, having obtained an unlimited supply of cigarettes from a wrecked NAAFI, was tossing cartons around, shouting 'Here we are, lads, all free and with the compliments of the NAAFI!'

Seeing a damaged Spitfire gliding inland with flames and smoke pouring from its engine, fired on by soldiers with a machine-gun, Deere ran like a demon to stop them but the noise of the gun drowned his voice, and as the soldiers finally realised their mistake the angry words that boiled up in his throat died away when he realised he could hardly blame them after two weeks of constant hammering from the air.

Guardsman Eldridge had now reached the perimeter. By the end of the previous day when the forward regiments were ordered to fall back, the 3rd Grenadiers, from being 1,000 officers and men strong, had shrunk to 9 officers and 270 men. Still pressed by the Germans, they had made minor stands as they withdrew down the long road past Poperinghe, hampered all the way by refugees.

Now, on the morning of the 29th, with the battalion split up, Eldridge found himself with one other Grenadier and a group of about eighteen

Engineers under the command of a major of the Royal Artillery, whose name he never learned but to whom he gave the highest accolade, true praise indeed from a Guardsman, that he was 'a real leader'. They made a stand at Poperinghe and another just outside the perimeter to allow troops to pass through them. Finally, blowing a bridge behind them, they reached Dunkirk. There were thousands of vehicles on the front so, instead of heading for the water's edge, they began systematically to destroy them so the Germans would not have them.

On the perimeter, Bombardier Sills' battery was being thinned out as men were sent back and there were now only sixty-four men, officers and specialists to serve the four 6in howitzers shelling Hondschoote and Bergues, flashing through the dust and smoke in a complete absence of cover and plotted all the time from half a dozen enemy observation posts at once. A steady drizzle now set in, and on the beaches men waited in groups, huddled in greatcoats and groundsheets, the water dripping off their helmets. Their faces were grey with fatigue and tense with expectancy as they waited, helpless, patient, but always hopeful. Among them was Gunner Hammond, whose commanding officer, Major Guy Cubitt, a hunting enthusiast, used his horn to rally his men.

Some of them were in the shallows cooling their aching feet, their boots round their necks. Some tried to make rafts from driftwood; others, in vest and pants, were preparing to swim. Some, indifferent to the noise and wrapped in overcoats or looted eiderdowns from wrecked houses, snatched the first real sleep they had had for three weeks. Some forced their way into the hotels along the promenade, still shuttered from the winter, in search of water or food. There was so little water they were driven to drinking from lavatory cisterns, and the only food available was what they had brought with them. They could not even *buy* food. The shops were also shuttered and they had no money because the field cashiers had long since been sent home.

Bodies appeared to be scattered everywhere, but as the light increased these turned out to be abandoned greatcoats. The air was filled with the stench from dead cows and horses. Whole groups of French cavalry chargers had been abandoned on the beach, wheeling and galloping about in terror as the Stukas screamed down and the bombs fell away. Those which had been hit had been lying in the sun for three days now.

Reaching the mole just as another attack developed, pilot Alan Deere saw soldiers on the beach diving into the water to reappear neck-deep and fire their rifles at the attacking bombers. Moving without interruption to the head of the queue, he was stopped by an Army officer. Dirty, bloody and unshaven, Deere tried to explain that he was trying to get home so he could rejoin his squadron and get back into action.

The officer was having none of it.

'For all the good you chaps seem to be doing,' he said, 'you might just as well stay on the ground.'

Far from being a small man, with the physique and features of a boxer, Deere told him to go to hell. Nevertheless, he joined a queue and, finally climbing aboard a destoyer, was greeted by a stony silence from the Army officers in the wardroom.

'Why so friendly?' he said. 'What have the RAF done?'

'That's just it,' he was told. 'What *have* they done?'

Deere was staggered. 'I had flown my guts out,' he said, 'and that was all the thanks I got.'

He still had not finished either. With the destroyer under air attack all the way to England, he was called to the bridge to identify aircraft. 'We think the last chap we had a go at,' he was told apologetically, 'was a Blenheim.'

Still waiting in Dunkirk, Sergeant Gough saw an officer with a lorry-load of champagne which he was handing out to anyone who wanted it. By this time Gough's unit had shrunk almost to nothing. From a deserted chemist's, he somewhat guiltily extracted a toothbrush. In another deserted shop stacked with shoes, one of his men was pretending to be the assistant. 'Yes, sir?' he asked Gough, rubbing his hands in the accepted manner. 'What can I do for you?' Gough's boots had worn out so he replaced them with a pair of Alpine boots. Despite this, there was a surprising resistance to looting and little was taken beyond what was desperately needed.

During the afternoon the 6,900-ton *Clan MacAlister*, the largest vessel to appear at Dunkirk, was bombed. She had been carrying landing craft so that the Army could do something to help themselves and, as she got them into the water and was taking on her first loads of men, she was hit and set on fire. A third of her crew and many of the soldiers who had just boarded her were killed or burned to death. As HMS *Malcolm* took off the survivors and the wounded, Captain R. W. Mackie, her master, decided to take his ship to sea. She had barely moved, however, when she was attacked again and this time had to be abandoned, burning fiercely. Her red-hot hulk became a landmark for the ships coming into Dunkirk during the following days.

As she burned the pall of smoke from the town and the oil tanks was drifting over the harbour, but then the wind changed and the Luftwaffe caught a whole flotilla of ships moored alongside the East Mole, jammed in hard against each other so that it was impossible to manoeuvre or get clear. Two big paddle-streamers, *Fenella* and *Crested Eagle*, were on the east side of the mole. Against its inside face were the destroyers *Grenade* and *Jaguar* with six trawlers further inshore.

Astern of these was the personnel ship *Canterbury* and further in were the destroyers *Malcolm*, *Verity* and *Sabre*. The French destroyers *Mistral* and *Siroco* were at the guiding jetty and at the Quai Felix Fauré was *Cyclone*. They made a perfect target and the searching Stukas split up into sections at once and plummeted down on the mass of shipping and men.

Fenella was loading stretcher cases from the quay and had almost 700 men on board when she was hit by a bomb which passed through her deck, killing many soldiers. A second bomb hit the mole, to blow pieces of concrete through her side below the waterline and flood her engine room and wreck her pumps. The troops began to disembark at once and, despite the constant bombing and machine-gunning, her entire load of men, including stretcher cases, was transferred to *Crested Eagle*.

Grenade, with a direct hit on her depth charges, was an inferno of flame just opposite and, as her mooring lies parted, she swung into the fairway out of control and for a while seemed in danger of blocking the entrance to the harbour. With ammunition exploding through the crippled ship, a trawler managed to tow her outside and she was barely clear when she went down. Some of the men swam ashore and a drifter picked up the others, only to be sunk in her turn and fling them into the sea again.

Two of the trawlers were also hit and literally disintegrated. *Canterbury* and *Jaguar* were badly damaged but managed to struggle clear, *Jaguar* being later abandoned but refusing to sink. Of the French ships—the first to arrive since Weygand had finally taken the decision to evacuate—*Mistral* had her superstructure smashed by blast and flying metal which caused heavy casualties.

Completing the embarkation of survivors and crew from *Fenella*, *Crested Eagle* had just slipped her lines when she was also hit. She was an oil-burner and, blazing furiously, she headed in to the beach at Malo-les-Bains. On board was Private Cornford, the officers' mess cook, firmly under the impression by now that they had been embarked to go to Boulogne to rejoin the fighting further south.

After being bombed and shelled on the beach, he had been directed to the mole and had finally scrambled aboard as the attacks developed. Ships were trying to close *Crested Eagle* to take off her survivors but the tremendous heat drove them back. As the ship settled, men began to jump overboard, and Cornford and other survivors scrambled over the side and fell into the sea among the bodies and floating debris and began to fight their way to the beach they had only just left. Swimming and wading, helping to pull or carry the wounded, Cornford finally crawled up the sand and flopped down in the shallows to get his breath back. Behind him, *Crested Eagle* was already a red-hot hulk, and bodies charred or covered with oil, floated round her in the moving tide, watched by the bedraggled and exhausted survivors huddled on the beach with the burned, scalded and wounded they had dragged ashore.

Despite the disaster, the armed boarding vessel *King Orry* still tried to get in. She had already been bombed and set on fire on the way across, but the fire had been put out and it was decided to make the attempt. As she entered, a direct hit on her stern wrecked her steering gear and she swung out of control against the mole, putting it temporarily out of action. On the other side of the mole, *Fenella* was a wreck and *Grenade* was still blazing furiously. As *King Orry* smashed into the mole, tearing a gap in it, the destroyer's magazines exploded and she was riddled with fragments and showered with pieces of metal, stone and wood. As her crew struggled to clear the debris, it was discovered that her rubbing strake had come to rest on one of the timbers of the mole as the tide had gone down, and it took two hours to get her clear. Her officers had been intending to beach her but suddenly, in the early hours of the next morning, she listed to starboard and sank.

With the harbour blocked, evacuation switched back to the beaches. At La Panne, Colonel Viner, the beachmaster, had long since given up all hope of getting any sleep. At high tide, he beached Dutch skoots and barges full of rations and ammunition, which, as they settled, were unloaded by a working party of Guardsmen. The French on the beach at this point were in a poor state, some of them panicking, and on one occasion he was nearly shot. British discipline remained excellent, however, and there was no queue jumping, although one lieutenant-colonel of a Territorial artillery unit snapped suddenly and pushed ahead of his own men. Viner stuck his pistol into his stomach, called a military policeman and ordered him back to his place. Another officer arrived with golf clubs, tennis rackets and several trunks.

'What are you going to do with that lot?' Viner asked.

'I'm taking them to England,' he was told.

'Over my dead body,' Viner said.

Viner had been on the beach a long time now and another lieutenant-colonel was sent to replace him, but as he arrived they were attacked by a German plane. Viner saw the bomb falling, shouted a warning and flung himself down. The bomb blew his replacement into a crater from which he was rescued suffering from concussion and sent home on a stretcher.

When Trooper Gillam of the 12th Lancers arrived in La Panne, with a transit camp in the surrounding woods and GHQ in the nearby chateau, there were soldiers, lorries and a surprisingly large number of staff officers with their cars parked everywhere. As shelling started, everybody dived for cover and he saw the missiles land in the ornamental pond of GHQ, sending a spray of water into the air with lumps of concrete and clods of earth. He was very proud of his regiment. To other regiments, the 12th Lancers were 'The Dirty Dozen' and to the infantry 'The Manure Collectors', but they called themselves 'The Supple Twelfth' and considered themselves—with some justice—to be 'quicksilver'. He noticed that, though some troops had thrown away their rifles and equipment, some—among them the cavalry—had everything.

The air attacks were still causing havoc and, with the RAF fighting further inland, at Dunkirk there seemed no answer to them. The Southern Railways' ship *Normannia*, hit by a bomb, settled on the bottom in shallow water and on an even keel so that her masts stuck out above the surface, the signal flags still flying. Soon afterwards *Lorina*, another Southern Railways' ship, was hit amidships and broke her back. Watching from the shore, Gunner Hammond saw a man flung hundreds of feet into the air by the explosion. Then the paddle minesweeper *Gracie Fields* was caught as she left La Panne and circled at six knots with her rudder jammed and her engineers unable to stop her. The men on deck were scalded by escaping steam, but despite everything, two skoots managed to get alongside and take off troops. The minesweeper *Pangbourne*, which already had dead and wounded strewing her decks after a bomb hit, managed to pass a tow rope, but *Gracie Fields* was too badly hit and finally settled on the beach where Viner made use of her as a pier.

Waverley, a Harwich minesweeper full of troops, had her rudder ripped off and her wardroom flat wrecked by bombs, one of which went through the bottom of the ship. Within minutes of the order to abandon, she sank, and her captain, Lieutenant S. F. Harmer-Elliott, found himself surrounded by a mat of struggling, shouting, drowning men. The first ship to reach them was a French destroyer, followed by the personnel ship *Golden Eagle*, drifters and a tug. Between 300 and 400 men died.

Despite the disasters, ships' crews were behaving magnificently, and their captains were acting with great initiative. *Waverley's* flotilla mate, *Oriole*, was run on the beach by her captain, Lieutenant E. L. Davies, and men used her as a pier to other ships in deeper water astern of him. Three thousand troops passed over her to safety and Davies finally took her off with a load of 700 soldiers and nurses from the last of the field hospitals. When he came to submit a report, he made no bones about hazarding his ship. 'Will again run aground if such a course seems desirable,' he wrote.

The Germans had committed both their air fleets in the west to the harbour, and the pounding of the perimeter and the retreating armies had virtually ceased. The RAF had doubled the size of its patrols, however, against 19 RAF fighters lost, 65 German planes were claimed, though the Luftwaffe recorded only 18.

Curiously, from where Dr Epps sat at Bray Dunes, it had all seemed surprisingly calm. He was eight miles from Dunkirk, and arriving as the light faded, he was unaware of the seriousness of the situation. He had been dive-bombed on the way and at one point had left it almost too late because he had mistaken the crank-winged Stukas for Lysanders, which also had odd-shaped wings and spats over the wheels. Although he had not felt nervous, the bombing had given him an appalling dose of indigestion which he diagnosed clinically as caused by fright. Now, waiting on the beach, he saw hundreds of lights in the darkness and immediately thought the Navy had arrived to pick them up. It turned out to be phosphorescence in the waves breaking along the shore.

The losses in ships this day had been horrifying and, knowing that the destroyers, more than any other type of ship, were needed to protect Britain's life-lines, Admiral Sir Dudley Pound, the First Sea Lord, ordered all the modern ones out of the action. It left Ramsay with only fifteen older vessels.

One of the lucky ones was the ship that pilot Alan Deere had boarded. She had escaped before the disastrous attack of the afternoon. As she berthed at Dover, Deere dodged the people directing him to a canteen and caught a train for London. Still filthy and wearing a bloodstained bandage on his head, he fell asleep only to be awakened by an officious ticket collector who insisted on a ticket. Having taken off as usual without money or any means of identification, he was told he would have to get off at the next stop.

Before he could reply, a brigadier sitting opposite joined in. 'It's obvious the boy's telling the truth,' he said, 'Can't you see he's all in and anxious to get back to his unit? How do you suggest he does it—walk?'

The brigadier, Deere thought ruefully, obviously had not heard about the RAF at Dunkirk.

Deere was one of the 47,310 men landed in England during this day. Despite the disasters it had turned out to be a triumph.

THURSDAY 30 MAY

When morning came on 30 May, the line of the Dunkirk perimeter ran along the Bergues-Furnes canal. The French held it from the sea in the west to Bergues, a matter of 11 miles, and the British for 21 miles from Bergues to the sea in the east. Outside now were only stragglers and the troops holding Bergues and the outskirts of Furnes. From the front line, the towers, chimneys, cranes and spires of Dunkirk were clearly visible, but although the nearness of the sea gave comfort, it also indicated that breakthrough could be disastrous.

Since leaving the Escaut, the 7th Guards Brigade had passed though crowds of soldiers of three nationalities, all leaderless, some panic-stricken, some even mutinying or helping the Germans. The roads had been packed with vehicles and, while the Germans suffered no such congestion, the British were becoming muscle-bound for lack of space. As the Guards reached Furnes, half the town was in German hands. Street fighting was taking place among the blazing houses, and brigade headquarters on one occasion was a slit trench dug through the middle of a manure heap, with a straw and dung roof for camouflage. When several officers were hit by sniper fire, Second Lieutenant Briggs was ordered to take his anti-tank Hotchkisses into the town and shoot up a house from which the Guards were being enfiladed. Although the Hotchkisses were not much good for tanks, he found they were excellent for houses, the missiles passing through brickwork with ease.

The news that they were to act as rearguard at Dunkirk was conveyed to James Langley's group by Brigadier Beckwith Smith, commanding the 1st Guards Brigade, a high-spirited man who regarded it as splendid news and a supreme honour. He then instructed them how to deal with the Stukas they might meet. 'Take them high like a pheasant,' he said, and offered £5 to anyone who brought one down. He had already paid out £10.

After heavy fighting at Rugge and St Eloi, the Duke of Cornwall's Light Infantry had just slipped inside the perimeter, having fought rearguard actions all the way back. Nieuport was being heavily shelled and eighteen-year-old Corporal Ronald Candy, who had given a false age and joined up at sixteen when his parents had died, noticed that the sky was full of flashes and flares. Just outside the town they had dug in around an empty farmhouse inside which an old Cornish reservist known as 'Happy Horace' was cooking two ore three chickens he had caught, in a stewpot in the huge open fireplace. When the shelling had started, one of the missiles had hit the chimney, shaking down soot into the pot, and, unconcerned with the fact that he might have been killed, 'Happy Horace' rushed out in a furious temper, shaking his fist in the direction of the Germans. 'You've spoiled my stew, you bastards,' he yelled. 'If I get hold of you, I'll bloody well kill the lot of you!'

Private Morphy's group of the Royal Sussex had also reached the perimeter. The previous day they had also taken over a farm where some of them were led to a ploughed field and told to dig in. The field was stony and they had no spades, so they used their helmets to scoop at the soil. Morphy's hole, he decided, was just about big enough to conceal his respirator.

That night, German infantry and tanks passed them, but they were so outnumbered they could do nothing but lie low. On the morning of this day, 30 May, they made their way to a hill from which they saw dozens of abandoned British lorries and spiked guns in the valley beyond. Finding a truck which worked, they drove it until it ran out of petrol, then started walking. French soldiers with commandeered civilian vehicles gave them a lift, and it was from these men that Morphy first heard the word, 'Dunkirk'.

Fifteen miles from the coast, they started to walk again. To Morphy, they seemed to have been marching all over France, and he had agonising blisters on his feet. Outside Dunkirk, they passed a big bonfire where soldiers were putting their vehicles into gear, letting in the clutch and jumping clear as they rolled into the flames.

Far to the south where Cassel had finally fallen, Corporal Wernham and the remnants of the 4th Ox and Bucks were trying to make their way back to the British lines. Their defence had been one of the finest feats of arms in the campaign but, with darkness and with many men killed, including the colonel, they were told it was every man for himself, and they had moved off in the dusk to cut their way out. With them were the 2nd Gloucesters and the 1st East Riding Yeomanry who had shared the battle, and throughout the night they had fought their way steadily back until they were split into small groups. Wernham's group cleared the enemy with a bayonet charge and soon after dawn found themselves near a wood. Deciding the

Germans would inevitably have occupied it for cover, they began to circle it, only to discover their mistake at once. The Germans had *not* occupied the wood and they ran into them. After a scrambling fight which brought more casualties, they were obliged to surrender. As the white flags went up, Wernham threw his rifle bolt into a pond.

That morning early, GHQ reported to the War Office that the perimeter was not expected to hold for long and asked that as many boats and as much ammunition for the anti-aircraft Bofors guns as possible be sent over. In fact, the Germans were preparing to withdraw for the attack against Paris and out of all the immense forces at their disposal only one worthwhile attack was made against the British troops. Against the Guards, it ran into a determined opposition but on the left of the Guards a badly mauled battalion of a county regiment was driven back. The commander of a Guards carrier platoon halted the retreat, dismounted his men and himself led the counter-attack which drove the Germans back across the canal.

The line continued to hold but Ramsay, also informed that it was likely to break, realised that with only fifteen destroyers in addition to the other vessels he possessed, he could reckon on lifting no more than 43,000 men altogether. He also had no idea whether the mole was functioning again or not and had to send in the destroyer *Vanquisher* to find out. The weather had improved, however. The drizzle of the previous day had stopped, the surf had gone down, and there was a low hazy cloud ceiling, while drifting smoke was again screening the harbour. Moreover, the Channel, that most notorious of stretches of water, remained unbelievably calm, and no full-scale air assault developed.

More and more small craft were streaming in to the beaches now in a weird armada of all shapes and sizes. To help them the Army was building piers with trucks, Bren carriers and ammunition waggons run out into deep water. Major-General H. R. L. G. Alexander, of the 1st Division, was one of the first to hit on this idea and it was taken up all along the beaches by the beachmasters.

At midday, to his dismay, Gort was informed that he was to return to England after nominating an officer to take over when his army had been so reduced it could be commanded by a corps commander. 'On political grounds,' Churchill's orders stated, 'it would be a needless triumph to the enemy to capture you when only a small force remained under your orders.' It was also decided, on Churchill's urging that the French should be given an equal opportunity to escape, not only in their own vessels but in British ships.

Ramsay was now informed that it might be possible to hold the perimeter until early on 1 June, by which time the BEF would be reduced to a rearguard of about 4,000 men, and it was agreed that the bridgehead should be diminished by narrowing it from east to west by the progressive withdrawal of the remaining troops. Having appointed Montgomery to relieve him, Brooke was also under orders to return to England under a scheme to get the experts home to rebuild the Army.

As the light increased, a breeze sprang up. It prompted a welcome relief from the bombing as it carried the smoke across the harbour. Unfortunately, it also hampered the small boats working on the ebbing tide, but real organisation was appearing now and parties were being given numbers so they would move to the boats in the correct order, while a cordon of men with bayonets diverted French troops to the harbour where an officer with a loud hailer chivvied them on.

There was still some waste of effort at sea, however, but gradually Rear-Admiral W. F. Wake-Walker, who had been appointed Senior Naval Officer afloat at Dunkirk, brought order to the work. At 4 am he had transferred his flag from HMS *Esk* to the fleet minesweeper *Hebe* but, with *Hebe* filled with men, he transferred his staff to HMS *Windsor*, and for himself used a motor torpedo boat from which he later switched to the minesweeper *Gossamer* and from her to *Worcester*. As *Worcester* also filled with troops, he transferred his flag once more, this time to *Express*. Despite the changes, he kept the ships coming in and seven destroyers landed more than 1,000 men each at Dover.

French destroyers were also busy. *Bourrasque* picked up between 700 and 800 men and was on her way to Dover by Route Y when she struck a mine. The torpedo boat *Branlebas* put boats into the water and, although overloaded, picked up 100 men. Two drifters picked up more but, as *Bourrasque* sank, her depth charges exploded and killed many of the men in the water. Of those who were picked up some were so injured it was hard to see how they managed to swim.

Dunkirk was burning fiercely now, the smoke depositing a layer of fine ash and cinders on the water, which was already black and greasy with patches of oil from sunken ships and aircraft. As daylight came Dr Epps, sitting in the dunes five miles from Dunkirk, noticed his rucksack was covered with greasy black spots of soot from the oily smoke overhead. Though he could hear firing and saw a ship at sea hit and disappear in a great blast of flame, things still seemed extraordinarily quiet where he was, and there were no casualties, no hurry and no hysteria.

Nearer to Dunkirk, however, machine-guns were going constantly and the sea was flecked with small plumes as the bullets struck its surface and the shell splinters came singing down. The hospital ship *Isle of Guernsey*, with 490 wounded on board and shaken every few minutes by the explosion of bombs, had to pick her way through a mat of struggling men from a sunken transport. It was a difficult decision for her master, Captain Hill. The men were drowning, yet, because of the ship's size and the perfect target she made as the flames picked out her white paintwork, he dared not stop.

Navigation by this time was becoming extremely difficult because of wreckage, upturned boats and inexperienced soldiers trying to paddle collapsible boats with rifle butts. As they were picked up, many offered the sailors cash or personal belongings in gratitude. They were usually told to send a postcard if they got home all right. None of them remembered.

With several large Carley floats in tow, each containing about fifty men, the Southend pleasure boat *Shamrock* had her propeller fouled by one of the many floating bodies and had to be abandoned. She represented her owner's life savings and the only thing he could think of doing was praying. To take the places of the vessels that were lost, fresh ones were constantly arriving, their owners, many of them civilians, showing tremendous initiative. When one group found they could not get far enough in to reach the troops, one of their number, *Lansdowne*, was run ashore and used as a pier, before finally leaving with a full load of her own.

At 6 pm Gort held a conference at La Panne. It was decided that First Corps was to form the rearguard, which, he had been informed, was to leave in equal numbers with the French or, if necessary, to surrender with them. Churchill, who had just been to Paris to see the French Premier, was determined to do nothing to harm the alliance. Wondering who to nominate as his successor, Gort had originally chosen Lieutenant-General Michael Barker, of First Corps, but Montgomery said that what was needed was a man with a calm, clear brain who, with luck, might even get First Corps away. He suggested Alexander.

Alexander had done well in the fighting. The 1st Division, like Montomery's 3rd, was a good one. As one officer said, 'Everything worked. There were no flaps', and its commander had been fighting on familiar ground, because he had marched the Irish Guards from Mons in 1914. Above all, as Montgomery had suggested, he was completely unflappable. According to Brooke, he gave the impression of being oblivious to all the very unpleasant potentialities of the Army's predicament. 'He remained entirely unaffected by it, completely composed, and appeared never to have the slightest doubt that all would come right in the end.' Gort did not hesitate: Alexander was selected.

That evening, Wake-Walker, going ashore with Tennant to make contact with Gort, discovered to his surprise that there was a view that not enough was being done to get the Army off. It was indicative of the strain everybody was under that it was Brigadier Oliver Leese, normally a large friendly man with an easy manner, who made a remark about 'the ineptitude of the Navy'. The trouble, of course, was that the Army had no conception of the Navy's problems.

Horrocks, having just brought his Middlesex men inside the perimeter, was summoned to 3rd Division HQ and arrived to see Brooke handing over to Montgomery. For once, Brooke—like many officers leaving their units—was emotional. His shoulders were bowed and he looked as if he were weeping, while Montgomery was patting his back in sympathy.

Now in command of Brooke's corps, Montgomery handed over his 3rd Division to Brigadier K. A. N. Anderson, of 11th Brigade, who was replaced by Horrocks. Horrocks had been in command of a battalion for exactly seventeen days, in action every bit of the time. Searching for Anderson, he found him eating bully beef in La Panne. Anderson indicated the positions held by his regiments, then departed to take over the division. Horrocks managed to find the battalion HQs and visit one or two companies but that was all, because next day 11th Brigade was ordered to withdraw to La Panne to embark for the UK. 'I doubt whether any brigade commander ever made less impact on his brigade than I did,' he said.

Guardsman Eldridge and the group with the artillery major had spent the night in an empty house on the front and now, with daylight, doggedly started destroying vehicles again. Dr Epps, moving to Dunkirk with his driver, a dentist and another man, came under shell-fire for the first time. But even now, as a shell landed near him on the mole, it did not explode but merely went off with a fizz and a shower of sparks. He eventually boarded the destroyer *Whitehall* and was startled when he reached England to discover the situation. Although later involved in heavy fighting with the Guards in North Africa, in France he had seen no action and no casualties at all.

Nevertheless, although he had thought he was unaffected by the dive-bombing, later when sitting in a field in England attending a lecture, he looked up and saw a cloud of gnats circling above his head. His first reaction was 'Good God, they're bombing us again!' and dived to the ground. His original unit, the 1st Field Ambulance, reached England without the loss of a man, but their commanding officer, swimming out to find a ship for them, climbed aboard just as it left, so that, to his disgust and fury, he was carried away without his men.

By now, Sergeant Gough of the Royal Engineers had decided he would never get away. His last job had been to gather what was left of his unit. There were zigzag lines of men down the beaches among the dead and dying, and the place stank to high heaven. Offshore, ships were awash and burning and on the beach one of his officers, Lieutenant Hubbard, was trying to rescue rowing-boats flopping about empty in the surf. His men had been rowing troops out to the ships all night.

When Second Lieutenant Street's company marched through the town, there were a lot of dead British soldiers lying about and the few remaining French civilians were angry because they would not bury them. Reaching the beaches and seeing the enormous numbers of men, it seemed they would never get aboard a ship, so they handed the captain's bulldog and the two spaniel puppies they had carried with them from Belgium over to men who had managed to get a place in a queue. He suspected all three were shot by the quarantine authorities as soon as they reached England. Hundreds were, and hundreds more which had attached themselves to soldiers and followed them right across France, were shot near the mole by their new owners to prevent them starving.

Young Trooper Gillam had spent the night on the beach. There had been constant air raids and at first light he saw two ambulances full of wounded blow up. Two jetties had been built out into the water from 3-ton lorries and there were boats alongside them, with, further out, destroyers, Isle of Wight ferries, even dredgers. He waited half the day, standing with the water up to his chest, moving forward a little at a time. Every time there was an air raid the boats sheered off and the destroyers moved further out. With Gillam were two other men, one smaller than he was who could not swim whom they had to hold above water until a boat came. When it arrived, manned by a young naval lieutenant, an elderly stoker and a young sailor, there were thirty or forty men on board. It was the old stoker who seemed to be giving the orders.

'Git in,' he said. 'We're going home. Straight over there.'

Two hundred yards offshore, the boat started to sink but when the water was up to their chests, they were picked up by a larger boat and finally ended up on a dredger manned by civilians and naval men. They could not sleep because of the air attacks, but Gillam remembered that the Navy knew about evacuations. 'You'll be all right,' the naval officer had hold him, and he believed him implicitly.

In England a new spirit was growing, compounded of defiance, relief that the army was being rescued and a belligerence at the knowledge that now nothing could save the country but its own efforts, ingenuity and courage. Rafts small enough to be manhandled and ladders to load small ships from the mole or to pick up men who had waded out to grounded ships in the shallows were being built, and a constant stream of small craft was being sent across. London, Dover, Newhaven, Portsmouth and Southampton all sent their quotas. At Portsmouth, the 34,000-ton battleship *Nelson* which had been mined off Loch Ewe the previous year, had just come in after repairs. Arthur Shuter, an eighteen-year-old ordinary seaman, had just joined her when the desperate need for boats arose. Every power boat the ship carried was put in the water and Shuter found himself with three other men on the admiral's barge heading for Dunkirk.

These small vessels lifted troops both from the beaches and from Dunkirk itself. HMS *Bideford*, a 1,105-ton sloop, had just boarded French colonial soldiers and 400 Lancashire troops from Bray Dunes when she was struck by a bomb. Forty feet of her stern was blown off, 75 men were killed or wounded and she ran aground. Surgeon Lieutenant John Jordan stayed in the sickbay and dealt with the casualties, many of them horribly mutilated, performing several major operations, with the aid of a private of the 6th Ambulance who had just embarked.

Soldiers who had rushed on deck were reassured by the crew that there was no immediate danger of sinking and *Locust*, a shallow-draft river gunboat half *Bideford*'s size, came alongside, took off many of the soldiers and took *Bideford* in tow. During the attempts to dislodge her from the sandbank, every available man formed up on one side of the ship then rushed to the other and back again to rock her free. She eventually floated clear on the rising tide and for thirty-six hours, all through 30 and 31 May, *Locust* wrestled with her yawing wildly from side to side in the stream of traffic, with the French colonial troops on board loudly insisting that they be taken back to France and the British being organised to tackle them in the event of mutiny.

RNLI lifeboats were also arriving but, as exhausted soldiers trying to reach them were knocked over in the shallows and drowned, it seemed almost to the crews that they were doing more harm than good. Boats were also being swamped and some of the naval ratings manning them, often drawn straight from training establishments, were not skilful enough under the prevailing conditions. The crew of the Ramsgate lifeboat took their places and, arranging for the soldiers to wade out in small groups, conveyed them to the lifeboat and other craft.

At Dover, fifteen other lifeboats arrived from as far north as Great Yarmouth and as far west as Poole. They were far from ideal for the job and when the first crews protested that they would be stranded by a falling tide, Ramsay's officers did not argue—the crews of the first three boats were replaced by naval crews. To the indignation of the crews that followed, naval crews took their places, only the mechanics being retained.

As this was happening, Robert Hector, the survivor from Norway, finally learned what was going on. On arrival at Dover Castle, all three-badge men like himself were told they were coxswains and he was given a second class stoker who had never been to sea and knew nothing about engines and an ordinary seaman straight from a training establishment. They drew rations of loaves, bully beef, tea and sugar and were taken to Dover Harbour. He chose the Dungeness lifeboat, and a stoker petty officer who had served on the royal yacht said he had picked the best of the lot. 'Two engines,' he observed. 'I wouldn't mind coming with you,' He was promptly roped in.

With five other boats, they moved to the mouth of the breakwater and were taken in tow by a tug. After only ten minutes, to Hector's surprise, the tow was cast off. The skipper of the tug shouted a course and left them to it. As it was pitch dark Hector put the lights on and they began to head south into the blackness.

Pickfords, the carriers, sent five ships; one of them, *Chamois*, after being beaten back twice by air attacks, rescued survivors from two ships that had been heavily bombed two miles off Dunkirk, many of them with their clothes on fire and the ammunition in their pockets exploding. Belgian fishing vessels, heading west to safety as their country was overrun, were diverted by the French Navy. They were all small, and the smallest, *Maréchal Foch*, actually sank under the weight of the soldiers who boarded her. Her crew salvaged her at low tide, reconditioned her and brought her back with 300 men on board.

The destroyers and cross-Channel steamers were still doing most of the lifting and it was clear to Ramsay that he had to have the big destroyers back. The men now appearing had held the Germans back for others to reach safety and not only did they deserve a chance to escape, they were needed to rebuild against invasion. He made his point firmly and that afternoon six H and I class destroyers were ordered back to Dover. With their arrival at Dunkirk the embarkation figures rose dramatically. As they did so, more senior Army officers left, their work now done, Adam and Brooke among them. Brooke was later critical of some of the arrangements on the beach and gave credit to the wrong man for what good work was done at La Panne. It was in fact Viner who had run the organisation there for four-and-a-half days, but he was wearing only a coloured forage cap, a leather jerkin and no badges of rank, and was probably overlooked. And it was Viner who, with a sergeant, carried Brooke out to a boat so he would not get his feet wet.

Among the small vessels working the beaches was the motor yacht *Constant Nymph*, belonging to Dr B. A. Smith of London. Unable to resist 'the opportunity of playing boats with the Navy', he had gone across of his own accord. Now he was moving along the shore, picking up French and English swimmers, waders, men on rafts and in small boats, and ferrying them out to larger ships. When a British officer waded out and informed him that a whole division was waiting nearer to Dunkirk, he began to ferry men to the skoot *Jutland*.

Other motor yachts were also arriving, many of them not in the best state of health after the winter lay-up. Oyster dredgers, ferry-boats and open motor boats followed, often bombed or under fire, and the soldiers came off the beaches clinging to pieces of wood, wreckage and anything that would float.

What was left of the Duke of Cornwall's Light Infantry had now reached the shore and began to march along it as a body, the idea being that if they were attacked by aeroplanes their massed fire would drive them away. But they made far too large a target and, splitting up, were told 'Every man for himself'.

Waiting in the dunes with two other men, Corporal Candy watched a soldier moving about collecting abandoned water bottles and taking them from the dead until both arms were full. He wondered what he was up to until he saw him ram the corks home in the empty bottles and string them round his chest as an improvised lifebelt before wading off into the sea.

The first French troops who came to the water's edge seemed unable to understand that boats could be overloaded, and many were flooded and sank. The 24-foot *Eve* was one of those swamped, and her skipper, Leading Seaman Norman Furse, was the only survivor. Some skippers, however, had revolvers and forced the demoralised men to do what they were told. But the inland Frenchmen, some of whom had never seen the sea before, had no idea how to behave and could not grasp that too many of them in a boat could ground it so firmly nothing on earth would move it until they climbed out again. Flung out by furious sailors, they stood in the shallows, working themselves into a passion of fury as they shouted for help. General Sir Edward Spears, Churchill's military liaison officer with the French government, summed up the inland Frenchman's attitude to the sea: 'I suddenly realised,' he wrote, '. . .that to them the sea was much the same thing as an abyss of boiling pitch and brimstone, an obstacle no army could venture over unless they were specially organised colonial expeditions endowed with incomprehensible powers.'

A few of the British soldiers spent the time waiting by digging shelters and roofing them with the bonnets of abandoned vehicles. A few disintegrated morally and merely sat waiting for capture. Others patiently read or slept and one group of youngsters sat listening to an older soldier reading from the Book of Common Prayer. Others regarded the defeat with the air of cynical disillusionment and mocking self-deprecation that was the stock-in-trade of all British servicemen. One officer noticed how extraordinary well-mannered everybody was, as though it simply was not done to make a fuss. Corporal Candy found he was not afraid and later, when he was an old enough soldier to be careful, he could only put it down to being too young to realise what might happen to him.

The imperturbable Private Morphy spent most of the time asleep. Reaching La Panne, the Royal Sussex had been divided into groups of thirty and, while waiting, he had dropped off. When he awoke, he found the other twenty-nine had disappeared. For a while he wandered about, firing his rifle occasionally when German planes came over. Then he joined a queue, only to be told they were West Kents and to go and find his own queue. When he could not find the Royal Sussex he went to sleep again.

Still the ships came. The pleasure boat *Princess Maud* was hit in the engine room as she arrived on her second trip but her crew plugged the hole with mattresses, and drained tanks to heel her over. She was able to return to Dover under her own steam. *Prague*, a cross-Channel ship which had first left Dover on 28 May, picked up so many men in the harbour she grounded and it took the efforts of two tugs to refloat her. The hospital ship *Dinard*, loaded with wounded, got away with her captain using an electric torch to pick his way around wrecks.

Late that evening, Gunner Clark of the 98th Field Regiment went out once more with Lieutenant Blades on the dangerous job of spotting enemy targets for the gunners. Once more they ran into the Germans but this time they were not so lucky. Discovering German half-track vehicles in a sunken road, they decided to knock them out with hand grenades. But as the grenades went off Clark and Blades found themselves bolting across the field with the Germans in hot pursuit. Reaching a ditch, they dived in and Clark heard Blades, who was just behind, give a yell as a German poked him in the backside with a bayonet. It was the end of the war for both of them.

As darkness came, several boats were run down in the confusion, and the surface of the water became littered with every kind of wreckage imaginable that had floated up from the sunken ships, to say nothing of bodies and upturned dinghies. There were even floating torpedoes from the previous night's attack. The town was a shambles too by now, littered with broken vehicles, dead horses and dead men, lying in the grotesque attitudes of death, eyes and mouths wide open 'like dogs that had been run over'. They were in the streets and in gardens and houses. Stretcher-cases covered the whole ground floor of some houses in the town.

Lance-Corporal Warner, the military policeman, who had spent the day sheltering in bomb craters, noticed like Dr Epps that the surf at the edge of the sea was surprisingly phosphorescent and it made him feel very vulnerable. When he reached the mole it was fairly clear and the men moved swiftly along it. Then a medical officer, strained to the point of appearing demented, started screaming 'Stretcher bearers!' Being a military policeman, Warner, like everybody else, did not think it meant him and nobody moved until the doctor made it clear he was asking for volunteers.

As a tug came in he jumped into it and was later transferred to the destroyer *Whitehall*. As they were pushed below they were told they were quite safe because the deck was bomb-proof. It clearly was not but it was reassuring to hear from the Navy that it was.

The weariness was beginning to show. Many of the sailors working the ships broke down and collapsed from sheer exhaustion. Nevertheless, 53,823 men were lifted this day, almost 30,000 from the open beaches.

FRIDAY 31 MAY

Robert Hector, in the Dungeness lifeboat, arrived off the French coast at daylight on 31 May. The night had been very dark and as daylight came he saw that other boats which had left with him had all disappeared. He decided to go in nevertheless, but everything seemed so quiet where he was, he decided it probably was not Dunkirk anyway. Then, 2 miles offshore, a flotilla of destroyers appeared on their quarter and started to bombard the coast over their heads; convinced, Hector abruptly about-turned and picked up a new course to arrive finally at the Dunkirk breakwater. An air raid was taking place and the whole area seemed to be full of French and British soldiers. The civilian coxswain of a boat near him decided not to go into the mole, but Hector, with the straight-forward thinking of a man with years of naval discipline behind him, considered it his duty to do so.

On the first trip he could not pick up many men because the deck was still filled with cans of extra petrol, but he kept on all day feeding ships outside the harbour. Then, while they were alongside the pier, the engines cut. As they were towed off, the stoker petty officer got one of the engines going again and from then on, they decided, they would operate on one engine and keep the other in reserve once it was repaired.

With his brigade ordered to La Panne, Horrocks had established a control point at Coxyde and as the last unit disappeared through it, he followed them. La Panne was being shelled and bombed all the time and, expecting that most of the troops would already be on their way to England, he was horrified to see the beach covered with men. Viner's piers had been constructed out into the sea by this time but the tide was right out and there were no boats—not even rowing-boats—anywhere near them, although away in the distance he could see ships. Fortunately, the sand seemed to absorb the shell and bomb splinters and although the situation was clearly desperate, the casualties were not as high as he had expected.

Going to the headquarters of General D. G. Johnson, of 4th Division, to his amazement he found Johnson speaking direct to the War Office in London. 'This is not a very healthy place,' he was saying, and he held up the telephone to pick up the din outside. Obligingly, at that moment a shell burst on the roof with a resounding crash.

Johnson was on the point of moving his division to Dunkirk and he ordered his officers to set them off on the 10-mile march along the beach. A lot of men had taken shelter from the bombing in the cellars and Horrocks was given the job of routing them out.

Shortly after sunrise, the wind changed and, as it increased in strength, the surf rose again in the shallows. It was never much but it was more than the weary soldiers and the exhausted men in the boats could handle. Boat after boat grounded. The first were pushed off again but, as the tide began to fall, there were small craft ashore all along the coast. Then, as the smoke was dispersed by the breeze, the German artillery found the harbour again. In the smoke and flying spray from the explosions, Robert Hector was careful never to remain stationary alongside for long, knowing that a hit with the amount of petrol they had on board would send them sky-high. More and more accurately, the fire began to drop in the loading berths, and at the other end of the perimeter at Nieuport, German guns were now shelling the La Panne beaches, controlled by an observation balloon beyond the Yser.

Reaching Dunkirk, the 7th Guards Brigade Anti-Tank Company had parked their vehicles along the front—'just as at Brighton, except that they didn't have to pay'. The harbour reminded Second Lieutenant Briggs of Shoreham, except that there were bodies on the mole and dead horses lying about.

They mounted their Hotchkisses in sandbagged emplacements on the beach and promenade in case the Germans attacked at low tide, then, finding some anti-aircraft Bren guns, began to take part 'in a partridge shoot against the Stukas'. The company commander offered 10 to 1 they would not hit anything and, though they peppered a few, he took their money.

Behind them, with the Guards Brigade still holding the canal, James Langley watched a continuous stream of British and French troops passing through. They varied from a leaderless rabble to a platoon of the Welsh Guards who had been in the fighting at Arras but managed to look as though they had performed nothing more arduous than a day's peacetime manoeuvring. One corporal of the Buffs excited his admiration. Barely 5 feet tall, he had a Bren gun slung on each shoulder with a rifle resting across the barrels. The slings of the Brens had cut deep into his shoulders, his back and chest were caked with blood, and Langley could see part of both his collar-bones. Langley offered him a cup of tea and told him to put the guns down as he would need them himself. The corporal refused. When ordered to drop the guns, he still refused. 'My major's dead somewhere back there,' he said. 'His last words were "Get those guns back to England, they'll be needing them soon." And begging your pardon sir, I'm going to.' Langley put a generous measure of whisky in his tea, placed first-aid dressings under the slings and wished him luck. The French who passed were very different. Finding themselves under British protection, they flung their weapons into the canal and said that the sooner France surrendered the better.

By this time, for his 37 men Langley had collected 12 Brens, 3 Lewises, 1 Boys anti-tank rifle, 30,000 rounds of ammunition and 22 Mills bombs. He considered he was fairly well off for fire power. They were also reasonably comfortable and well supplied with beer, wine and food. Warned to fire on all low-flying aircraft whatever their markings, he got in a good burst at a Lysander with a Bren. Fortunately, he missed, because he heard later it contained Gort who was having a last look at the final line.

Gunner Bain, after having spent some time dug in on the beach, had now reached the mole. Pieces had been blown out of it and there were bodies everywhere, but with other men he lined up and they stood 'as if on parade' motionless under the strafing. He had not had a decent night's sleep for three weeks and his feet had been so swollen with driving, he had often taken off his boots and socks to operate the pedals.

The East Surreys had also reached the beach, Private Hersey's new French wife always jolting just ahead of them in the company commander's truck. Now, as Loveland and the others went on to the sand, drivers were called for to bring in the rearguard. Although he was supposed to be a non-driver, Hersey had managed to drive his wife the last few miles in a truck after half an hour's instruction and he now felt he had to volunteer. Private Alf Pearce had found a portable radio in one of the houses and he and Loveland and a few others were trying to tune in to the BBC. Suddenly the programme was interrupted by the German propagandist Lord Haw Haw, the British renegade William Joyce. 'Troops of the BEF on the beaches of Dunkirk,' he said in his hated grating voice, 'I'm going to play you a tune.' It was 'We're going to Hang Out the Washing on the Siegfried Line', something which, despite its popularity at home, the troops in France had never liked. Now, in fury, Pearce took a flying kick at the radio just as an attack by Stukas developed, and as Loveland bolted for shelter, he saw Pearce hopping round on one foot, with the radio wrapped round his boot.

Private Cornford was also still on the beach, two days after being bombed in *Crested Eagle*. The ship's survivors had searched for food and water in the houses as their clothes dried, and now, as a ship came in, he queued in the water with men from every regiment in the BEF, finally being picked up in a small boat and climbing up a net hanging over the side of a ship. Lying against the far side of the vessel were several naval motor boats. 'Come on,' Cornford said. 'They'll probably be quicker.' So he and several others climbed down to the motor boats. As the boat they were on swung away and headed for England, one of the naval men said to him, 'I know what you poor buggers have been through. Well now you're going through a minefield!'

There was no food left anywhere in Dunkirk now and officers and men were eating from the same tin of bully beef and sharing the same biscuits and the same dregs of wine. Haggard, unshaven soldiers moved among the abandoned vehicles and houses in search of a forgotten tin or loaf or biscuit. Corporal Candy and his two companions from the Duke of Cornwall's were lucky. There were bodies all over the beach and at one point they saw a dead Frenchwoman with a child in her arms, crouched on the sand, both of them killed by machine-gun fire. The three soldiers were desperately hungry but they managed to find a box containing tins of Machonochie stew, the troops' standby, generally known as 'dog's vomit'. They had no tin-opener but they wrestled the tins open with bayonets and ate the cold stew with their fingers. To Candy, it was better than the best Christmas dinner he could remember. Other soldiers tried emptying the radiators of abandoned vehicles and making a small fire for a brew-up. But at the first salvo of shells, the first sound of areoplane engines, everything was dropped in the rush for the dunes.

Sergeant Gough, released at last from rowing troops out to the ships, was told to go to the mole. Fighter-bombers kept appearing, and men were killed every few minutes. As he reached the mole a bomb hit it. Planks were laid across the gap and he made his way towards a trawler and began to collect ammunition bandoliers to hand to the Bren gunners. When the ship left there were dead men lying the whole length of the pier. Like Cornford, he still could not believe they were going home and still felt they would be landed further along the coast to start again.

Aircraft continued to roar overhead and at one point they saw a parachute drifting down with a man beneath it. Although Gough did not fire, everybody else did, but the parachutist drifted through it all to fall into the sea, from which he was hauled on board. He turned out to be an RAF pilot and his disgust was monumental.

'What bloody poor shots!' he said. 'No wonder we're losing the war!'

As Gunner Bain climbed aboard *Royal Daffodil* among a lot of Frenchmen, near him was a young soldier of the King's Own Scottish Borderers. Only a handful of his unit was left after their defence of the perimeter near Bulscamp and the young soldier started running about, shouting in a panic. They tried to calm him but in the end they had to hit him to knock him out. Then someone gave Bain a swig of water with naval rum in it and he fell asleep. It was the anniversary of his wedding and, with a kitbag full of NAAFI cigarettes, it seemed a good way to celebrate.

In Dover, Ramsay had learned of the breakdown of the lifting from the beaches because of the wind. The moles were also desperately dangerous by this time and, not daring to concentrate too much shipping off the beachhead, he temporarily suspended sailings.

In fact, a great many men had already been lifted and, as the first figures came in, they were good enough for him to order his last small craft across. Gort had now amended his original estimates, and said that the final evacuation of the rearguard would be postponed until the night of 1–2 June.

Despite the successes, however, the day had begun with the loss of the French destroyer *Siroco*. She was hit by a torpedo near the Kwinte Buoy and, seeing the cloud of steam rising from her, the German bombers closed in. A bomb exploded the ready-use ammunition on the deck and two others hit her in the vicinity of the bridge, so that in a confusion of exploding shells she heeled over and sank. The Polish destroyer *Blyskawica*, which had just missed being torpedoed, went to her assistance but fuel on the water made the operation difficult and the loss of life was heavy.

As ships left Dover, more moved up to take their places. The master of the Southern Railway steamer *Hythe* went into Dunkirk with only an Army map to navigate on, and sailed with 674 men on board. She was followed in by another Southern Railway steamer, *Whitstable*, which had had to wait off Bray Dunes. Her captain was indignant that the destroyers came and went quickly while he had had to lay for hours in an exposed position; but the destroyers, old hands at the game now, knew just where to go and inevitably filled more swiftly.

The 800-ton store ship *Levenwood* was driven nose-on to the beach by her master, Captain W. A. Young, who kept steaming slowly ahead to avoid going broadside on. In this position he got a hawser ashore and, although bombed, sent in boats by it. One of his firemen kept going over the side and swimming to wading soldiers, encouraging them to strike out for the boats and helping those who were too weary to help themselves. He worked for three hours in the heavy swell of the surf.

New helpers were still coming across. Major J. R. L. Hutchins of the Grenadier Guards, in command of the War Department launch *Swallow*, soon decided it was a waste of effort to pick up men and take them straight home, so he spent the day ferrying to bigger ships. To increase the numbers, he took over a service cutter and, when it was rushed by soldiers, he instructed them how to distribute their weight and towed it, still festooned with men clinging to its sides, out of the reach of the remainder of the men in the water. Stopping until the soldiers, all very weak and helpless, were hauled aboard, he went alongside the destroyer *Impulsive* and, borrowing her whaler and two men, he made more trips to the shore. When *Impulsive* had to leave, he transferred to *Winchelsea*. Taking command of other launches and borrowing boats from the davits of a wreck, he continued to pick up troops so that, when *Winchelsea* left, he had transferred between 700 and 800 men from the shore.

The morning's losses had already been made good and now, with the new arrivals, came Thames barges carrying stores for the hard-pressed men on the beaches. Broad-beamed, shallow-draught vessels, as often as not they were crewed by an old man, a boy and a dog. One of them, *Lady Rosebery*, was hit before her stores could even be unloaded, and of her crew, a seaman and a boy of fifteen disappeared. But some got their cargoes ashore and some even got off again loaded with men. For the most part, however, to make sure, they were merely run aground and abandoned. After the evacuation one of them was found off Sandwich. Another was picked up in mid-Channel with 260 men on board. One motor-driven barge made her way home with 352 men and even did two more trips, bringing roughly the same number of men out each time.

All the time the tugs were bringing in damaged vessels and towing across trots of boats and lighters—even pontoons for bridge building—all loaded with food, water and ammunition. One of them, towing five RAF seaplane tenders, had them break adrift six times, but they all eventually arrived at Dunkirk where they rescued at least 500 men. The French were joining in now in numbers with forty-eight vessels—from destroyers to fishing-boats—working the beaches and harbour. By this time, communications from ship to shore were working well and the surf had died, and as the tide rose the makeshift piers fed men in large numbers to the boats. Following the RAF tenders came cockle boats from Leigh-on-Sea and the Dutch skoots, small squat ships with their diesel engines astern, which were perfectly suited for the job. They were also lucky and only one was lost. Ramsgate sent four hopper barges, designed to take the spoil of dredgers. Load after load of men were lifted by them and from one of them, RASC gunners shot down a German plane.

The ex-naval steam pinnace *Minotaur*, now a Sea Scout training craft, crossed with Scoutmaster T. Towndrow as skipper and a Rover Scout as engineer. They were astonished at the way the French soldiers refused to give up their equipment. It often required all the strength they possessed to get them on board. In the early afternoon the Thames fire float *Massey Shaw*, belonging to the London Fire Brigade, arrived. Little more than a floating platform for pumps, she had been sent in the hope that she might fight the fires in Dunkirk, but as it was obviously pointless to try, they ferried troops instead.

As the stream of small ships came in, German batteries at Nieuport tried to halt them. Trying to knock them out, Wake-Walker's latest flagship, *Keith*, was heavily attacked from the air, while *Vivacious* was hit twice and had several men killed or wounded. It was during this attack that Gort left, just as La Panne was coming under increasingly heavy shellfire. His car stuck in the sand, but a boat appeared and he was pushed aboard with Leese by Viner and ferried out to *Hebe* which was now picking up men from the beaches. Despite having the Commander-in-Chief aboard, she did not stop working and Gort took his chance like everybody else.

The beaches were now packed with men who had been forced nearer to Dunkirk as La Panne came under fire, and a naval officer sent to embark 5,000 men, found on arrival they had swollen to 20,000. The sight of a queue of 1,000 waiting for a single dinghy was dreadfully depressing.

The casino was being hit regularly every ten minutes with salvoes of shells, then the shells would fall along the water's edge for the next ten minutes. The men with boats soon learned to time their efforts and, as the shells fell with clockwork regularity, they went in as the casino was under fire then, filling up with men running from the dunes, pushed off before the firing was switched to the water's edge.

But is was never easy anywhere. Some of the men trying to climb into the boats were often numb with shock, hunger or lack of sleep, but the queues, often marshalled by padres, whose calm helped to keep order among the anxious men, were well organised. But for the men pressing out into the sea, the water, despite the heat of the day, was cold and the current swift and many of the tired men were soon in difficulties. Along the tide-line were the rows of the dead, left there neatly by the receding sea, while among the crowds on the beaches were shell-shocked, dazed soldiers wandering about trying to find some shelter from the bombing. A few dead men were buried in the dunes but the bombs disturbed the graves and in the end the dead were left where they were. Some of the men were even bomb-happy and on the edge of hysteria, while dozens of abandoned horses, still on the sand, were galloping about as the bombs fell, with the packs of terrified, starving dogs.

Everybody was working at full speed, however, and Second Lieutenant Street, still waiting for a boat, was impressed by the incredible calmness of one very young sailor throughout the bombing, shelling and machine-gunning. Little more than sixteen years old, he was trying to direct a motley crowd of soldiers, and nothing caused him to flap or lose his patience. The build-up increased quickly after dusk when the final withdrawal of Second Corps from the eastern sector of the perimeter began. There was a need for speed, because the withdrawal meant the Germans could creep 9 miles nearer, and that Bray Dunes would now come under shellfire, too, and eventually the beach at Malo-les-Bains.

Now in sole command, Alexander went to see Admiral Abrial and General Fagalde in the citadel. He was as calm as ever. At one point he was seen watching the battle from a deckchair and then moving among the troops munching an apple. He had arrived in Dunkirk on a bicycle because of the congestion on the roads, his sole equipment his revolver, his field-glasses and his brief-case. He was still unaware that Churchill had committed him to evacuate the French in equal numbers with the British. It was Abrial's idea still that only 'specialists' were to leave, but Alexander explained that the situation was such that it was inviting collapse to try to hang on longer than necessary. Abrial was calm but, since by noon on this day 144,000 British had been landed in England against 15,000 French, the French view was that the British were only able to escape because the French were still fighting. Going to La Panne, Alexander contacted Eden by telephone. Eden said that 50–50 meant from that time on, not from the beginning evacuation as Churchill had said in Paris. Even then it was difficult. Abrial thought it meant according to the numbers engaged which, since there were still 120,000 French to 20,000 British, would have meant lifting six Frenchmen to every Britisher.

In the end Alexander decided, like Dowding with the RAF, that it was pointless committing any more to the lost battle in France when it was necessary to build up forces in England against invasion. When he communicated his decision to the French, Fagalde was furious. 'But Lord Gort placed you under my orders,' he snapped.

'Lord Gort is now at sea,' Alexander said calmly. 'I alone am responsible for British troops still in France. If we remain here another 24 hours we shall be taken prisoner. I have decided to re-embark without delay.'

Contacting the War Office in the last communication before the telephone link was cut, he was heard by Brigadier Dempsey to say quite firmly, 'I just don't propose to hold beyond Sunday night. After that we're all coming home.'

'Thank God,' Dempsey thought. 'There's a man who is in control.'

When the weary Private Morphy awoke this time, he found the beach had emptied a lot, so he walked on his own into the sea. An Army padre appeared with a rowing-boat and pulled him aboard with a few others and rowed them to a destroyer. Put in the bowels of the ship, they were just settling down when there was a colossal bang but immediately a sailor arrived to reassure them with the usual dose of 'whoppers'. 'It's a British ship firing,' he announced and, though they guessed it was more likely a near miss from a bomb, they were happy to accept the explanation.

Guardsman Eldridge, still with the Royal Artillery major's group, waded out to a fishing smack converted to a minesweeper and was dragged on board, still in possession of all his kit. They were given bully beef, bread and cocoa, which they wolfed with the haste of men who had not eaten for four days.

Gunner Hammond also made it to a ship this evening from the mole. He had been very much an amateur soldier at the beginning but by now he had become tremendously impressed by the value of Army discipline. There was still no rushing and the men moved forward two or three steps at a time, watching the head of the queue gradually disappearing seawards. Not a man stepped out of turn and, eventually, he scrambled aboard a destroyer. Although he was crammed below deck, for the first time, with all the steel around him, he felt secure.

He was so tired in fact, he did not care whether the ship was bombed or mined, or whether it went up or down.

Private Loveland had also made it to a paddle-steamer, but for Private Hersey it was more difficult. Finally given permission to join his wife, they struggled through the deserted streets to the beach where an Army beachmaster immediately turned Mrs Hersey back. In desperation, she was fitted out with khaki trousers, while an Army captain added a greatcoat, and they slipped into a queue along one of the improvised jetties. Everybody was too tired to notice and they finally climbed aboard the destroyer *Ivanhoe* in the closing hours of the day.

Still the boats chugged among the shallows. Sometimes the men aboard saw the soldier they were reaching for simply sink out of sight with exhaustion. His agonised eyes beneath his helmet vanishing as he was unable to make any effort to save himself. One officer wrote how he saw a soldier standing asleep just ahead of him in the queue simply disappear. 'One minute he was there, the next he was gone.' The men on either side were so weary they remained quite indifferent.

In the dark streets of the town the men of the rearguard were now beginning to arrive, the broken glass 'crunching under their boots like ice'. They trudged through the burning Place Jean Bart and down the Boulevard Jeanne d'Arc, still in good order but too tired now to do anything but put one foot in front of the other. Behind them, other men were still working in the vast car parks just outside the town destroying everything they could find, and artificers were attaching 50 yard lengths of signal wire to the triggers of their guns, into which they had placed two shells, one in the breech, one down the barrel so that the gun would be shattered. Others were scattering cordite from cartridge cases on the grass so that any unwary German stopping for a quiet smoke after they had gone would find himself surrounded by a sheet of flame.

Having cleared the cellars at La Panne and got everybody moving towards Dunkirk, Horrocks found the beach had emptied, so he set off at the tail of the column. As he rounded the headland he had his first sight of the little ships—rowing-boats and motor boats suddenly appearing out of the dark in the shallow water 50 yards offshore. In their eagerness to get aboard, the soldiers overturned many of them.

They remained quite amenable to reason, however, when told what to do, and Horrocks arranged for an officer to stand on the beach while he himself waded into the sea and flashed a torch shorewards whenever he wanted a group of men to be sent to him. He kept the boats coming in to meet them and, by making the soldiers climb in carefully, a large number were taken away. Standing in the sea for a long time gave him cramp, however, and no matter how many men got away the beach always seemed to be packed.

For Robert Hector in the Dungeness lifeboat the day had been full of incident. The raids had seemed to come continuously, all of ten minutes' duration with a five-minute spell between them, the German planes arriving like clockwork until dark, after which he was able to work uninterruptedly.

The soldiers were mostly in good spirits. 'Where have you been all this time?' they kept saying. 'Didn't you know there was a war on?'

With memories of his uncompleted survivors' leave in his mind, Hector replied indignantly, 'This isn't the first evacuation *I've* been in.'

Despite the tragedies, the day had been a triumph, and when Gort finally stepped off *Hebe* and left with Leese for England in the motor boat MA/SB 6, Dunkirk was beginning to look less like a disaster; 68,014 men were landed this day, 23,000 from the beaches alone.

SATURDAY 1 JUNE

In the hours of darkness on the morning of 1 June, the whole front of Dunkirk was a high wall of fire, roaring with tongues of flame, the smoke pouring up in thick coils to the black sky. Men still trudged down to the beaches, a lot of wounded among them now, the blood bright on their bandages, the last regiments to pull back from the perimeter.

'Gun Buster', at last on the beach, tacked himself on to the rear of the smallest queue and, as the men in front clambered into a boat and were rowed away, they all moved forward until the water rose to their waists. His description of his own feelings was a description of the thoughts of every man on the beach.

His only wish now was to get into a boat. Not a word was spoken and the men just stood there, silently staring into the darkness, praying that one would soon appear, yet afraid that it would not. Soon only head and shoulders were above the water and the dead weight of waterlogged boots and clothes pinned them down. Trousers, ballooned out with water, seemed as heavy as mercury, and they were filled with a dread that when the time came they would not be able to move. Then came another dread—that they would stand there throughout the night and then have to spend the next day on the beach after all. The depression and the weariness of the wait was appalling and half of them were asleep standing up, waking occasionally with a start. Gradually they dropped the burdens they were carrying because they did not have the strength to carry them for another minute, and during the whole time, German shells continued to rain on the town behind them and stray splinters hissed into the sea. A quarter of a mile to their left, they could see tiny figures of men on the mole silhouetted against the flames of the town.

Then out of the blackness a white shape materialised into a lifeboat. It moved towards them and stopped 20 yards away. As they edged forward—until the sea lapped the chins of the shorter men—a blind urge drove them on, whether they could swim or not. Four sailors began hoisting them up but it was not easy because of their saturated clothes and because in their exhaustion they could do little to help themselves. The sailors judged the situation perfectly, using rough words, threats and bullying, which were sufficient to rouse the weary soldiers to one last effort. 'Gun Buster' gripped the gunwale of the boat with his fingers but when he tried to haul himself up he found he could not move an inch. Then two strong hands fastened on him and another pair grabbed the back of his coat and he pitched head-first into the boat.

'Come on, you bugger,' one of the sailors said. 'Get up and help the others in.'

The words meant nothing except relief.

'. . . A great burden of responsibility seemed to fall from my shoulders,' he wrote. '. . . I felt that my job was over. Anything else . . . was the Navy's business. I was in their hands and had nothing more to worry about. There and then . . . an indescribable sense of luxurious contentment enveloped me.'

At sea, the day had started well with the embarkation reaching new heights. Though La Panne had been abandoned, every man who could be found had been embarked from there by the previous midnight, the military chaplains almost always among the last to leave. Belgian trawlers were now working near Malo-les-Bains and two of them, despite their small size, carried away between them 1,500 men. Destroyers, minesweepers, skoots, drifters and paddle-steamers added to the total. All night the Germans had dropped flares to bomb the harbour and now, as the sun rose, they came again and began to machine-gun the beaches. Barges were still running ashore with supplies and at 7.20 am, as soldiers ran towards them, the guns started again and they had to dive instead for shelter. This attack was to be one of the most devastating of the whole evacuation. There were no Allied aircraft about and the destroyers were short of ammunition.

Daylight had found what was left of the 6th Black Watch on the beach at Bray, where an improvised jetty had been built. Unfortunately it was low water and the ships were too far out. Two horses were found but when optimists tried to swim them out to the ships, the horses, 'had more sense than their riders and weren't having any'. Split up into parties of forty, the Black Watch marched eight more miles to Dunkirk, shot up on the way, before they finally felt the deck of a ship under their feet. Four regimental police on a raft paddled themselves with rifle butts out to a ship and one very young second lieutenant marched his platoon along the mole singing the song the regiment had sung for generations:

'. . . Of a' the famous regiments that's lyin' for awa',

Gae bring tae me the tartan o' the Gallant Forty-Two'.

The colonel managed to reach the destroyer *Keith* just as she was attacked. Down to her last thirty rounds of ammunition, there was little the ship's captain could do except take evasive action, but as she turned to port nine bombs fell in a line along her starboard side, heeling her over on to her beam ends. Her rudder jammed, she began to turn in tight circles, and as she did so a second attack came in and a heavy bomb went down her after funnel to explode in her boiler room, while near-misses damaged her hull. Enormous clouds of steam rose as she listed to port, but then she seemed to steady herself. Admiral Wake-Walker switched his flag yet again, this time to MTB 102, but before tugs could reach *Keith* she was hit again and this time turned turtle and disappeared. Close by, the minesweeper *Skipjack* was also hit while lying at anchor, taking on troops. Ammunition began to go off like fireworks, then she was torn by a terrific explosion. She sank like a stone and only a handful of the 275 men on board survived.

On board *Ivanhoe* the Herseys' troubles were not yet over. As she went to the aid of a Thames barge, she was hit by a bomb and came to a dead stop, the decks hidden in clouds of roaring steam. Mrs Hersey, helping with the wounded in the sick-bay, was caught in a shower of breaking glass. Fighting their way to the deck, the Herseys found a minesweeper already moving alongside and, struggling with the soldiers to the rails, Mrs Hersey was helped aboard by an officer of the Royal Fusiliers.

With two destroyers hit, the bombers scented victory and were diving to within a few hundred feet of the water. *Basilisk* was also hit and the tug *St Abbs*, which had picked up the captain of *Keith*, Captain E. L. Berthon, who had taken the place of the captain killed at Boulogne, was hit amidships as she raced to the rescue. The colonel of the Black Watch, who had also been picked up, was wounded in this attack and was only saved from drowning by an elderly able seaman who gave him his own lifejacket. As *St Abbs* broke up, Captain Berthon, who had won the DSC at Zeebrugge over twenty years before, found himself in the water for the second time. As *Whitehall* began to sink, the hulk of *Basilisk* was also dive-bombed and suffered severe damage. *Worcester*, also damaged, began to struggle back to Dover, while the gunboat *Mosquito* had to be abandoned on fire.

As the raid had developed, men of the Duke of Cornwall's had been lifting stretcher cases on to a sloop and, sick of being shot at, they all started firing into the air until the ship's captain exploded from the bridge. 'Get those bloody pongoes below,' he yelled.

'They're shooting away my aerial!' It did not have the slightest effect on the firing.

Corporal Candy, who was still on the mole, saw a small vessel come alongside but, because of the low tide, no one could get down to it. Someone found a plank and, resting one end on the deck and the other against the mole, they slid down it one after the other until the deck was full of men. As the boat moved away, crammed with soldiers, they were caught by a German fighter and, with nowhere to hide, there were a lot of casualties. The boat stopped, but the crew managed to get the engine going again and they set off once more for Dover.

Horrocks had also been caught up in the holocaust. As dawn had broken, he had walked, wet and tired, to Dunkirk, 'a very temporary brigadier, with no staff and no troops'. There were still thousands of men on the beach —'like an immense khaki-clad football crowd'—and as German aircraft appeared there was a fusillade of fire which did not appear to do much harm, although it helped morale a lot, then everybody started to cheer wildly as the RAF came streaking in from the sea. His one fear was that the panzers would appear.

Horrocks arrived in Dunkirk just as the first big attacks were developing. There was the most appalling din from anti-aircraft guns, but he was too tired even to look up and he noticed nobody else looked up either. With other men, he was marshalled along the mole by a lieutenant-commander who also clearly had not slept for several nights, and eventually found himself in the unbelievable comfort of the wardroom of a destroyer where he was given hot rum and milk.

It was not over, however, and he heard a sickening crash as the ship was bombed. As she began to heel, he scrambled to the sloping deck, but two other vessels were already manoeuvring alongside, and he climbed on to a small Dutch cargo vessel commanded by a cheerful young naval lieutenant and already bulging with troops. 'Can anyone fire an anti-aircraft Lewis?' came a shout from the bridge and Horrocks manned the forward gun. It was the only part of the withdrawal he enjoyed. They were constantly attacked and he fired many magazines without visible effect, but for the first time had no responsibility and he felt it was a wonderful relief.

General Molinié, who had put up such a splendid fight at Haubourdin, had been forced to surrender at 9 pm the previous day and now, as daylight came, 200 Zouaves, gaunt and tattered as scarecrows but accorded the honours of war for their gallant stand, marched out fully armed to the music of a German band, past the men who had defeated them.

The beach by this time was becoming a distressing sight. Wounded, burned and blinded men waited silently, knowing they would drown when the tide came up. In some of the bomb craters dead men lay, head-down the fine sand slipping in rivulets from the lip at every bomb burst to cover their bodies.

Major Colvin, commanding the 2nd Grenadiers, had arrived on the beach to find there was no one to tell him where to go. What few boats there were, were kept for the wounded, and despite the air attacks, officers and men worked up to their necks in the sea getting them away.

Eventually, a destroyer signalled to them to move westwards to Dunkirk. 'It was an amazing sight,' he wrote, 'to see . . . thousands of men trekking across the sands . . . a solid mass five miles in length and about one hundred yards broad.' Messerschmitts attacked periodically and many were wounded and left to die. Picking up their own wounded, the Guards tried to find boats, but as they had all been perforated by bullets or splinters, they waded out to a grounded ship, tired and cold in their wet uniforms, only to see *Keith*, the destroyer they were hoping would pick them up, bombed and abandoned.

Eventually a string of boats came in and Colvin and his group got aboard one of them. They expected to be machine-gunned but the Germans were too busy trying to kill *Keith*'s sailors struggling in the oil-covered water. When the boat's engine failed, they tried to row and eventually reached an Amiralty tender picking up swimming men who were being carried along the coast on the tide. Most of them were almost dead with cold, all were coated with oil and many were horribly wounded.

In command was Captain Berthon, of *Keith*, who, as *St Abbs* had broken up, had swum clear with other men. They had been missed in the confusion by a small yacht and, after swimming for a long time, Berthon had managed to stagger ashore where he found the tender into which he got survivors from *Keith* and *St Abbs*. To Colvin, they seemed in a terrible plight.

An RAMC doctor was trying to help, aided by a padre who told Colvin, 'I have never prayed so hard before'. Attacked again and finally hit by a bomb which wounded Colvin, the tender heeled over. 'I remember a horrid feeling going down and down into a bottomless pit.' Colvin wrote. 'I took a deep breath, said a short prayer and . . .

had the sensation of being pushed through the water at great speed, everywhere surrounded by coal.'

Struggling to the surface, he found many men had disappeared and decided that most of those soldiers not killed by the bomb must have drowned each other in their struggles in the water. Carried by the tide towards a wrecked ship, he discarded his Sam Browne belt and wished he could do the same with his boots. Grabbing a rope ladder that was hanging in the water, he found that, because of his wound, he could not get aboard and had to let go, but finally he managed to struggle up a gangway. Eventually sailors found him a bunk in the deckhouse and gave him blankets and dry clothes, and, still under a hail of bombs, began to unearth tinned pears and biscuits from the ship's stores.

The long channel of the roadstead was full of wreckage, smashed boats, empty rafts and splintered planks floating among the huge pools of oil and the mats of bobbing corpses—of soldiers, sailors, civilians, even occasionally a woman. In just over an hour the Navy had lost three destroyers, a fleet minesweeper and a gunboat, and four destroyers had been damaged, while soon after midday the French destroyer *Foudroyant* was hit as she came in through Route X and capsized instantly. In addition, the cross-Channel steamer *Prague* which had been doing stirling work ever since 28 May, was attacked. A coal burner, she did not have the advantage of being able to go quickly alongside an oiler to refuel, but had to take all her fuel aboard from coal hulks and bunker laboriously with bags and shovels, every member of the crew joining in.

The transport *Scotia*, hit by five bombs, began to list heavily, sinking by the stern. With several of her boats smashed, the French troops aboard, not understanding the orders and knowing nothing of the sea, tried to rush what were left but the chief officer, using a revolver given to him by a Frenchman, got them to do as they were told. The destroyer *Esk*, skilfully handled by her captain, rescued many of the men on board but *Scotia* gradually leaned over until her forward funnel and mast were in the water, then, as she went over until her bilge keel came into view, those still on board huddled on the bilge until they were hauled to the deck of *Esk* by ropes. Between 200 and 300 men were lost.

The paddle minesweeper *Brighton Queen* followed soon afterwards. Although almost half of the 700 French on board were killed by the bombs which hit her, on this ship they behaved well. The small ships suffered in equal numbers, and out of one convoy of four only one escaped.

James Langley and his Coldstreamers were still in position on the perimeter, with a machine-gun nest and observation post in the roof of a cottage. They had water to cool the Brens and beer for themselves and when dawn came and the mist rose, they were startled to find themselves staring at 100 or more unsuspecting Germans only 600 yards away in a field of corn. The resulting massacre made him feel sick. When the Germans gathered a line of civilians, mainly women, and advanced behind them to pick up their wounded, good marksmanship still managed to account for several of them.

On a portable radio they had acquired, the Guardsmen listened on the BBC to an interview with a man who offered the disturbing information that he was the last man out of Dunkirk. As they listened, an officer from a line regiment informed them that the Germans were massing for an attack and that he was about to withdraw. He was ordered to stay put and told he would be shot if he did not. Then, in an old-fashioned way, they toasted the enemy. 'It seemed just like pre-war manoeuvres,' Langley thought. Preparing for a last stand, they punctured every tin of food they could find so the Germans would not enjoy them, smashed the kitchen stove, and continued to fire at anything that moved. Then, as Langley pushed another clip into his rifle ready for the next attack, there was a tremendous crash as a shell burst on the roof of the cottage to cover them with debris.

'Anybody hurt?' Langley asked faintly.

'No, sir, we're all right.'

'Well,' Langley said. 'I'm not.'

He had been wounded in the head, arm and leg and he was taken to Dunkirk by ambulance, lying beneath a man whose blood dripped continuously on to his face. By this time, there were so many wounded about they were taking up the places of the fit who might fight again, and the business of carrying the bulky stretchers aboard or rigging slings to hoist them up from the small boats off the beaches took so much time, individual decisions were reluctantly being taken that they must be abandoned. Langley was among the first to suffer. In the dunes, a man in a naval overcoat told him that unless he could get off the stretcher and walk the 200 yards to the beach he would have to be left behind. He could not and he was too tired to argue, anyway.

By the time Gunner Webb's unit reached the mole, it was badly damaged. Some of the planks laid across the breaches were not very thick and were springy enough to bend frighteningly as they picked their way along them. The news that *Crested Eagle* had been sunk bothered them. They were all East Enders and had often been on her from the Tower of London to Southend for the day, and the loss of this familiar vessel seemed to them to indicate the end of the world.

The word about the wounded being left behind was beginning to get about now, and Webb found the mole littered with bloody bandages torn off by men afraid of being refused permission to board. Alongside the fit there was also the bodies of men who had been killed there, covered with groundsheets or coats, and on the sand alongside, a grisly pile of them lay where they had been heaved out of the way.

Some of the men standing four deep in the queue, British on the right, French on the left, were actually asleep, muttering in nightmares but as indifferent to the danger as they were to the men pushing past them. A trot of six destroyers lay alongside but, when an air raid started, they all cut their lines and left. The French, all of whom seemed to be wearing blown-up inner tubes round their waists, were angry at the way things were going. 'The English have had their fair share,' one of them yelled. 'There should be one line of English and the rest French!'

One of the subalterns directing the boarding turned round. 'Take no notice of them,' he said to Webb. 'Shove the bastards in the sea.'

As Webb climbed aboard, the Luftwaffe arrived again and the destroyers' multiple pompoms started. The first aircraft was shot down as he was clambering to the outside ship of the trot. There were a lot of Frenchmen with him and they were so hungry when a sack of biscuits was produced they started fighting for them. He managed to get a place under the bridge where there were two scared Cockney conscripts from a Highland regiment who had been in a bayonet charge and they were still shuddering with shock. After a while, a hatch in the deck opened and the head of a sailor appeared.

'You don't want to mix with them French lot,' he said coldly. 'Come and have a cup of tea.'

With La Panne deserted, Viner had also finally reached Dunkirk. He had seen Brooke go and had now evacuated Gort and, after four-and-a-half days on the beach, bombed, shelled and machine-gunned, it seemed to be time to move. As he left, the beaches were coming under heavy shellfire, but he had taken the precaution of finding a car, filling it with petrol and hiding it in a garage, guarded by his batman. Now, as he drove to Dunkirk, there did not seem to be a soul near the piers and he saw no troops at all.

The British ports were working overtime. There was not a breath of wind or a cloud in the sky and the whole south coast was a scene of ordered confusion. The quaysides were full of red-eyed soldiers begging cigarettes, and dozens of barking dogs. As soldiers scrambled ashore, civilian helpers pushed aboard the ships with stretchers and first-aid equipment, and women began to pass round water bottles and telegram forms.

More women were working at mobile canteens with cups borrowed from local catering businesses, handing out food, calm despite the harassment from the men pouring ashore—senior officers mixed with private soldiers, French, Belgians, even an occasional German prisoner. The din was terrific, with loud hailers going as ships' captains demanded permission to moor, and, on one quay, a group of sailors yelling at French colonial troops they were accusing of stealing their kits. Men came ashore in little else but blankets or underpants, sometimes even in items of female underwear they had found in Dunkirk after they had stripped off their own clothes to swim from bombed ships. Some of them brought pets, some even presents for their families or girlfriends which they had bought for their next leave at home and had doggedly carried with them every inch of the way as if they had been returning from Blackpool. As they swarmed ashore, the ships' crews set to work to clear the dirt, the fuel oil, the pools of blood, and the equipment forgotten by the exhausted and stupefied men. On the quay, rows of stretchers waited for ambulances, and women—all too often in tears—bent over them fixing labels with names and addresses to the men's blouses.

The organisation was tremendous and there was no waiting. Along the known railway routes from Dover women prepared food and tea and collected cigarettes in village halls, station waiting-rooms and yards. But they reacted equally quickly where exhausted men were just dumped on them. At Rotherham, in Yorkshire, a horde of weary men stumbled from the trains and flopped down to sleep in the station forecourt. The women in the houses around had no idea who they were but when it dawned on them they were soon on the job with food and tea.

Among those who arrived in England this morning was Sergeant Gough. Out of his unit only sixty men had escaped. Gunner Bain, who had slept all the way across, was finally wakened by someone pushing at him with a boot. 'Want to look at England?' he was asked, and, sitting up, he found he was off Margate.

Trooper Gillam had also arrived at Margate where temporary canteens had been set up. Double-decker buses were waiting to carry them to the station but the regimental sergeant-major was having none of that.

'Oh, no!' he said. '*We march!*'

Everybody else went on the buses but the 12th Lancers, who had acquitted themselves so splendidly in the fighting, marched in threes with their arms swinging. It was a small example of regimental pride at work, that small thing which Gillam insisted made Dunkirk a success. They complained but they also put on 'bags of swank', and when an old lady offered Gillam a packet of fifty cigarettes, the RSM gently pushed her away. 'Leave him alone, Mum,' he said. 'This is Army business.'

Viner arrived on a paddle-steamer. Lewis guns had been erected on the paddles and, on the way over, to the great delight of the crowded troops, they shot down two aeroplanes. As he had left La Panne he had changed his battledress for his service dress because it was more valuable, and he had been careful to shave throughout the whole evacuation because, he said, he 'tried to look like a Royal Marine'. At Margate he went straight into a train and on the way to London even managed to clean his buttons. Stopping at a suburban station, he found parties of girls and Guardsmen appearing with trays of food. He was desperately hungry and when he asked for some, because of his smart appearance they would not believe he had just come from Dunkirk, and one of the Guardsmen told him bluntly to 'bugger off'.

Gunner Hammond was also bundled into a train and eventually arrived at Blandford where there were beds with sheets, something he had not so far seen in the Army. They were confined to camp for forty-eight hours and told to sleep, and it was the only time in his Army career that he had his breakfast brought to him. It was also there, however, that he realised that from being almost a non-smoker, he had learned to smoke twenty cigarettes a day.

Basil Bartlett, suffering from concussion and a fractured jaw, had arrived at Dover with fuel oil in his hair, blood on his face and full of the belief that Stevenson's observation 'to travel hopefully was better than to arrive' was a lot of nonsense. In hospital he found himself in the next bed to Lord Cowdray, whose shattered arm had had to be amputated and whom he had last seen in an ambulance in a line of vehicles just outside Dunkirk. A bomb had dropped close enough to blow open the door and re-wound the men inside. Supposing that in history the campaign would go down as a first-class military defeat, Bartlett himself was convinced, despite everything, that it was nothing of the sort.

It was an attitude that most of them felt, and there was a surprising amount of resilience and cheerfulness. Horrocks had not been looking forward to his arrival in England. 'We couldn't be said to have covered ourselves with glory,' he thought, but he was astonished to see cheering crowds, and immediately noticed the soldiers around him perking up and the letters BEF beginning to appear in chalk on the fronts of steel helmets as soldiers, even in disaster, kept one eye open to the main chance.

The reaction of the press to them was enthusiastic. Censorship had kept much of the news from the pages of the newspapers and, while the troops had been fighting for their lives in Norway, they had still been predicting big crowds at the summer holiday resorts. Even as late as 16 May, they had seemed as concerned with the Cup Final as with the war, and on 31 May the headlines had been full of the changes in professional football teams, although one paper did announce 'Sergeant Eager To Go Back'. He must have been the only man who was.

It was one of these papers that Gunner Webb picked up as he arrived at Dover, separated from his unit and with no idea what was happening. This feeling of confusion was general and to Webb, the Londoner, it was increased as he was stuffed into a railway carriage full of Yorkshire Bofors gunners, while the newspapers that were flung in after them showed a very different picture from the one he had just left. One of the Yorkshiremen was staring delightedly at the *Daily Mirror*. 'Christ,' he said, 'I thought we'd be shot for neglect of duty, but it looks like we're fucking heroes.'

Still they came, thousands of them, often stumbling ashore so weary they did not know what they were doing, their uniforms filthy and torn, their faces gaunt with strain. One group arriving at a West Country camp had been brought home in a coal barge and were so covered in coal dust they looked like sweeps. They had raw blistered feet and all too often fell asleep over the mugs of tea and sandwiches that were handed to them.

The ships that brought them often had their hulls holed by bullets and splinters, and carried bodies on their decks and blood in the scuppers. They arrived with their lounges, saloons, cabins, crew's quarters, even lavatories, crammed with men. With them they brought their own injured and sick, officers with feet so swollen with standing they could not get their boots off, seamen deafened by explosions, engineers scalded by ruptured steam pipes or stokers burned when flung by a wildly turning ship against a furnace door. Some of them were blank and stupid with exhaustion, so weary their legs would no longer work, often shocked by what they had seen and the number of dead. After the disasters of the morning, it was clear to Ramsay that it was impossible any longer to use destroyers or large ships during daylight, and sailings were discontinued. Without air support the thing was impossible. By this time the RAF was coming under heavy criticism, although, in fact, heavy fighter sweeps were being made. But assembling the squadrons took time and it was in the gaps between them that the heaviest losses had occurred. Every kind of plane was sent up, however, and at the end of the day they claimed 78 aircraft destroyed, though the figure was later trimmed to 43, while the Germans admitted 29, of which a number were undoubtedly destroyed by ack-ack fire.

Though it had been agreed that the evacuation should be completed by dawn on 2 June, it was finally felt that this was not possible and it was decided to continue until midnight, the rearguard withdrawing to a bridgehead round Dunkirk with every available anti-aircraft and anti-tank gun.

It was now that Bombadier Sills and his comrades of the 59th Medium Artillery were ordered to fire their last shells and destroy their guns. To reach the beach they had to march eastwards in pitch darkness for 4 miles in the direction of the Germans to the only surviving footbridge across the canal, then retrace their steps on the other side to Bray Dunes. When they reached the sea there was a lot of shelling going on, but their departure was well organised and there was no waiting. They waded into the water and were picked up by small boats which carried them to a minesweeper. Arriving at Margate, they were given stamped picture postcards of the town to write home, and Sills' wife, the daughter of a soldier and expecting a baby, saw it, picture uppermost, on the mat. Worried sick about her husband, she wondered who could possibly be enjoying themselves in Margate while the Army was fighting for its life.

With the Germans drawing nearer all the time, the windows along the Kentish coast were being constantly shaken by the thunder of the bombardment. Everybody going across the Channel now was well aware of what lay ahead. Yet still the small boats went and still the soldiers fought their way out to them on rafts made of planks and broken doors. Occasionally boats with dead engines were got under way again to tremendous excitement, and set off for home. 'I struck Dover dead centre', one able seaman recorded triumphantly.

As often as not the crews now had nothing to do with the boat they manned. Some had been forced to switch after being bombed or sunk. Others, many of them merchant seamen waiting for ships or ordinary civilians with seafaring experience, had been assigned without any pattern by the Small Vessels Pool to whatever was going across. When they were damaged or ran aground, the men scrambled ashore, climbed aboard another boat or helped to carry the wounded.

The 60ft *Sundowner*, owned by Commander C. H. Lightoller, who had been a survivor of the *Titanic* disaster, went across with Lightoller's son and a Sea Scout for crew. When 75 men had been packed below, every inch of space was used as more were crammed on deck. With 130 men on board, she returned to England where she was given permission to enter harbour at once. As the men poured ashore, a stoker petty officer, who was helping them, stared. 'God's truth, mate,' he said to Lightoller, 'where did you put them?'

Another man, Mr R. B. Brett, in charge of a tow of boats, saw what he thought was a pier, only to find it was a column of men, six abreast, standing in the water as if on parade. When he asked for sixty men, a sergeant stepped out smartly, said 'Yes, sir, sixty men, sir,' and detailed the first ten files.

Maid of Orleans, involved from the very first day, lay alongside the mole for six hours as a floating landing stage so that men could get from the high plankway to the smaller vessels, and eventually left with 1,800 men. *St Helier*, another of the first, though hit by shellfire, loaded wounded and, with every inch of space filled, managed to sail still under fire. Other ships which had been there since the beginning were also still lifting and *Royal Daffodil* brought back 1,600 Frenchmen.

Leaving the MTB which had picked him up after the bombing of *Keith*, Wake-Walker went into Dunkirk where he was informed by Alexander that he intended to continue the evacuation throughout the night from the town and the western beaches. But the night was dark and the gallant *Maid of Orleans*, which in six trips had lifted 5,319 men, was put out of action by a collision with the destroyer *Worcester*, which herself had lifted 4,350 in six trips. Fortunately there were plenty of vessels about and men flung into the water were quickly rescued.

It did not go so well for the crowded little boat which had brought Corporal Candy home. As she arrived she collided with a hospital ship and rolled over on her beam ends. Candy managed to grab the mast and hang on, but several Guardsmen, fully equipped and still carrying their weapons, were flung overboard and drowned—inside Dover harbour. Much of the trouble, of course, was caused by exhaustion. Some of the crews had been working solidly for a week now and could hardly stand, and Ramsay began to replace them with naval crews.

It had been a hard day too for Robert Hector in the Dungeness lifeboat and, as it drew to a close, down to their last few cans of petrol, he decided to leave before dark. He had nothing but praise for the young seaman in his crew, who had never lost his calm, placating soldiers who got into a panic at the bombing and yelling orders as if he had been used to command all his life. Hector himself also felt pretty good. The lifeboat had been his first command and he had found that even sergeants and officers had done as he had told them.

Just before dark, they hooked on to a buoy for a break. They had not been to sleep from the time they left Dover but they decided to do without for one more night. While they waited, the young seaman approached Hector. 'What's up with you, Swain?' he asked, and it was only then that Hector discovered he himself was wounded. Something had sliced open his chin during the last raid and he had been so busy he had not noticed.

Even as he replied, his chin seemed to lock and go numb, so they tried the rum from the first-aid locker. As they drank it, they realised they were hungry and began to open tins of bully beef. The loaves they had brought had all been given to hungry soldiers. The rum bucked them up and the young seaman tried to put a bandage round Hector's face and wipe down his oilskins which were covered with blood. A paddle-steamer full of soldiers towed them out as they let go of the buoy, and suddenly beginning to feel groggy, Hector let the young seaman take the wheel, and lay down. When the stoker petty officer told him they were on their way home, he finally went to sleep.

Between sunset on 1 June and dawn on 2 June, the remains of 46th Division, the 1st Division and 126th Infantry Brigade were taken aboard ship. Second Lieutenant Briggs and the Guards Anti-Tank Company came back on a destroyer and, since everybody else seemed to have gone, he decided they must be among the last out. The Brigade of Guards being 'well organised', they made a point of arriving in England 'washed, shaved and in possession of all their equipment', to say nothing of the anti-aircraft Brens which they had quietly appropriated. Since he possessed a pilot's licence and experience with gliders, Briggs soon found himself in the RAF where he ended up as a wing commander.

As darkness came, it was still the destroyers which were doing the major part of the lifting, among them *Whitshed*, repaired after being damaged at Boulogne. As she went alongside, the mole was empty and her captain, Commander E. R. Conder, walked along it, found a bicycle and rode into the town where he met exhausted British, French and Belgian troops, all of whom he took back with him. To make more space, *Whitshed* had unshipped all unecessary gear and now she even took the unprecedented step of leaving open her watertight doors to take 1,000 men aboard.

By this time, the orders were growing simpler. One convoy was sent across to 'pick up anything'. For the most part the ships remained in darkness or used dim navigation lights when threatened with collision. Among those picked up were Captain Berthon, Major Colvin, and the survivors from *Keith*, *St Abbs* and the bombed tender. Berthon had finally found a boat still on its davits on the wreck where they were sheltering and it was decided to try to row it across the Channel. Eventually, however, a lighter came alongside and as they climbed aboard they expected to go home. But the skipper of the lighter insisted on going in to the beaches where he picked up another twenty-five men. Even now, on their way home, they ran aground on a sandbank but managed to float off. The flowing tide reduced their speed to nothing. 'There was nothing to do,' Colvin said, 'but watch the bombers circling round.' But they were not attacked and when the lighter's engine broke down they were taken in tow by the tug *Sun XI* whose master had seen morse flickered at him by a very dim light. He thought the lighter, with its load of wounded and exhausted men, a 'terrible sight', and even now they had not finished. They had to stop twice more to pick up dinghies, one containing four Belgian soldiers and one containing two Guardsmen, and finally, packed like sardines, they were almost capsized by the wash of a French destroyer which arrived to investigate them.

It was full daylight as the last ships left Dunkirk and the Channel emptied. On this day 64,429 men were brought to safety.

HOME AND DRY

During darkness on the morning of Sunday, 2 June, Robert Hector, with his exhausted crew, following the reciprocal of their course to Dunkirk, saw something ahead of them.

'It's bound to be England,' Hector said, so they shut down engines and went to sleep without bothering to find out. Some time later a torch shone on them from what seemed a mile-and-a-half in the air. A vessel was alongside them and a disembodied voice was calling, 'You can't stop there. You'll be run down.'

Being run down after what they had been through seemed very unimportant. 'Tell him to get stuffed,' the stoker petty officer said. 'Where are we, anyway?'

They were just off Margate Pier so it seemed only sense to move in and, guided by the torch, they eventually tied up by a ladder.

'What's up with you?' someone asked, peering at Hector's blood-stained clothes.

'Nothing,' he said. 'Just tired.'

Nevertheless, an ambulance appeared, his chin was stitched up and he finally rode in style to the Winter Gardens where a soldiers' canteen had been set up. Unfortunately, though desperately hungry and with everybody about him eating, he found that with his sewn-up chin, all he could was sip a cup of tea.

It was clear it was almost over now, and the men still left on the beaches and still arriving in Dunkirk were beginning to wonder if they would make it. Alexander remained, as always, serene, polite and apparently unmoved. He used a large Humber limousine to visit the perimeter, invariably under heavy fire but always unflappable. When his driver, Corporal J. Wells, drove too fast, he slowed him down with the words 'They'll get you, Wells, whether you drive fast or slow. Better not add another hazard.'

He was saddened by the number of stragglers arriving without rifles but when the Grenadier Guards marched past and gave him an eyes-right, 'he returned their salute as if he had had a week's leave'. When asked by Tennant what he would do if it came to capitulation, he replied, 'How does one capitulate? I've never had to capitulate.'

Relations with the French were growing difficult now, although there was no reason for the resentment. Between 31 May and the last day, 98,000 Frenchmen were lifted against 20,000 British, which was much better than the 50–50 agreed on, and the Navy could have taken thousands more if only their organisation had been better. Often, while crowds of them waited on the beaches, in the harbour British ships waited in vain and finally sailed empty.

For the British still on the beach, a BEF chaplain celebrated Holy Communion but five times during the service the men had to scatter as low-flying aircraft appeared. There were still almost 4,000 of them ashore, and detachments fought alongside the French throughout the day. At 5 pm, a whole fleet of ships was ordered in and the French themselves sent forty-three. No more wounded could be taken off, however, and a last appeal by a signal in clear was made to the German command, requesting permission for hospital ships to enter. Soon afterwards, however, the hospital carrier *Worthing* was attacked, despite carrying all the markings required by the Geneva Convention, and the hospital ship *Paris* was badly damaged. Although tugs were sent, she was already sinking, and aircraft machine-gunned her boats, seriously wounding some of the nurses.

Under the circumstances, it was decided that one officer and ten men should remain with every hundred casualties. Names were placed in a hat, and that night the remainder of the medical men moved to the mole. Of the wounded who were left, many made valiant efforts, sometimes successful, to struggle to the ships. As daylight came, no more lifting was done, but destroyers, anti-submarine vessels and minesweepers began to work to make the channels safe for the night.

The perimeter continued to hold and at nightfall the flow of men to the ships began again, doggedly now, everybody knowing they were nearly at the end. The piermaster now was Sub-Lieutenant Wake because that afternoon Commander Clouston, who had worked unceasingly since the beginning, had been lost. He had returned to Dover for a brief rest and was returning with an augmented shore party when the RAF launch carrying them was attacked. As they took to the water, Clouston tried to swim to a boat about two miles away, but the week had taken its toll and, deciding he could not make it, he turned back again to the waterlogged launch and was not seen again. Under Clouston's direction, 200,000 men had passed down the mole to safety.

With the end so close, everybody was conscious of the need for haste and, in the dark, vessels were being lost in collisions or from shellfire, or even because water, put into petrol cans in the confusion in England, stopped engines. Propellors fouled on floating grasslines, equipment, coats and bodies, and many small vessels had to be towed away. The difficulties with the inland French were now at their height. Many still wore greatcoats and were festooned with rolled blankets, bottles of wine or brandy—even sacks of loot—from all of which they refused to be parted. Time was wasted as interpreters argued interminably with men reluctant to take to the sea, and from one boat came the unbelievable story of a French officer who refused to wade out into the water to a dinghy because he had just eaten.

Royal Daffodil, after her excellent work, was also finally put out of action. A bomb passed through three decks and went out through the starboard side. Everything moveable was shifted to the port side and the port boats were lowered and filled with water, which tilted the ship to that side and lifted the hole on the starboard side above sea level. Under the direction of the Chief Engineer, Mr J. Coulthard, it was stuffed with every mattress and scrap of bedding that could be found, then as she headed for Ramsgate, the Second Engineer, Mr W. Evans, stood up to his neck in water to hold open the bilge valve, while Coulthard kept the pumps going. A private of the RAMC worked alongside the wounded in a way that won him a tribute from the ship's captain.

The small ships were still crossing, and David Divine, who wrote the most authoritative of all accounts of the naval operations at Dunkirk, took over a small twin-screw Thames motor cruiser he had stolen, with Rear-Admiral A. H. Taylor, Operation Dynamo's maintenance officer, who wished to supervise the lifting of a pocket of men at Malo-les-Bains. The exhausted soldiers were staggering and weaving across the beach from the dunes into the water and literally falling into boats, and some of the bigger vessels were pushing in to them until they were almost aground. Yet, no matter how fast they were taken away, across the dunes came more hordes of men. The din was incredible and even the sky was so full of noise no one could speak normally. Everybody who was at Dunkirk developed 'Dunkirk throat', a hoarseness that came with too much shouting.

The last British of the rearguard appeared and the French began to arrive in a continuous stream. As the destroyers sailed, Alexander, with Tennant and half a dozen others, including Corporal Wells, boarded a naval motor boat in the harbour and, after ordering one of the destroyers to wait for him, zigzagged out through the gunfire and turned east parallel to the beaches for about two miles, as close as possible to the shore. Twice they grounded on sand-bars. The sea, Wells noticed, was covered with a film of oil, in which the bodies of soldiers floated. Alexander was using a megaphone, shouting over and over again 'Is anyone there?' and when there was no reply, they returned to the harbour, shouting the question again as they toured the quays. Finally they boarded the destroyer, and as they left Tennant signalled Ramsay, 'BEF evacuated'. The last ship to leave was *St Helier*, one of the first to appear off Dunkirk. She was fully loaded and it seemed that the embarkation had succeeded beyond the wildest hopes.

In fact, there were still 80,000 French ashore, 50,000 still holding the line. Twenty thousand of them were lifted the next morning in French ships, but, apart from the rearguard which had to be sacrificed, there were 10,000 for whom room could easily have been found. At 00.30 on 2 June, Wake-Walker signalled that there were four ships alongside the mole but no French troops, and at 1.15 am he sent 'Plenty of ships. Cannot get troops.' There had been a breakdown in the French command structure. The night was no worse than the preceding ones, but *Medway Queen*, which lifted one of the largest loads at this time, came away with only 723 men.

At midnight the total landed was 26,256, and soon after 3 am the next morning, blockships were ordered to seal the harbour.

The next day, Monday 3 June, broke in brilliant sunshine, but with the black smoke still lifting from the blazing oil tanks. The Channel was empty. In Dunkirk harbour, in addition to the wrecks, there was only the grounded French personnel ship, *Rouen*, anxiously waiting for a rising tide.

To the last boats to leave, the place seemed 'terribly lonely'. There were dive-bombers in the sky but there was no longer anything worth bombing. The Germans' final assault came between the Bergues and Bourbourg Canals. Counter-attacks were flung in by the French but their battalions were dwindling now and as they retreated again the Germans followed up.

Because of the sinkings and the damage, Ramsay now had only 9 of the 40 destroyers which had passed through his hands. Only 10 personnel ships out of 30 remained, and with their crews at the limit of their strength, he informed the Admiralty that if the evacuation was to be continued beyond the coming night, fresh forces would have to be sent. Yet preparations for the night were made. Destroyers, personnel ships, minesweepers, corvettes, a gunboat, drifters and motor-boat flotillas were readied, and the French produced 63 vessels. Together they were capable of lifting 30,000 men, which was the figure believed to be still ashore. In fact, 26,746 men were lifted, 20,000 of them French, all despite German machine-guns firing in the town. At times it was necessary to push, pull or bully the men on to the ships. Wake-Walker was still there, using a motor boat to move French fishing vessels occupying the berths the bigger ships needed.

As the troops scrambled aboard, the same personnel ships which had been doing the work all week were still at it, and *Royal Sovereign* brought away 6,858 men altogether. As the bigger ships worked the harbour, the small boats were searching for stragglers along the beaches and among the quays deep inside the town. One of them, the launch *Marlborough*, ripped off her propellers and rudder against a patch of rubble and was towed home by a motor yacht handled by a Dominican monk.

At 3 am, a French general and his staff were picked up by one of the last of the boats. There were still hundreds of men on the mole and they stood at attention while the general and his staff, 30 feet away in the boat, saluted them. The gallant *Medway Queen*, on her seventh trip, was rammed by a cross-Channel steamer but still managed to escape with nearly 400 French soldiers. The destroyer *Malcolm* raised her total to 6,400, while *Sabre*, the oldest destroyer at Dunkirk, pushed hers up to 5,000.

Admiral Abrial and his staff embarked in motor boats and the rearguard was successfully disengaged and the final retreat began with the understanding that the ships were waiting. Unfortunately, although the ships were there, hundreds of the places which should have gone to the rearguard were snatched from under their noses by men, both French and British, who had spent the whole nine days in cellars with no intention of helping in any way at all but who now appeared, determined not to be left behind.

There was one last tragedy. The French minesweeper *Emil Deschamps* which detonated a magnetic mine with 500 men on board, carried to the bottom survivors of the French destroyer *Jaguar* which had been lost before the evacuation began and whose crew had fought throughout as infantrymen. *Shikari*, one of the oldest and smallest destroyers in the navy, waited until dawn. She was the last ship out of Dunkirk, carrying 600 men.

There were still small craft about, however, looking for someone to take off, and from the admiral's barge of *Nelson*, Ordinary Seaman Shuter stared at the wreckage ashore. By this time, the crew was down to three, one of them having disappeared overboard after being hit by a stray bullet or a splinter. The boat moved along the beaches, its crew calling out 'Anybody there?' whenever they passed wreckage. The beaches were full of men but it was impossible to think of lifting them and suddenly for Shuter 'the penny seemed to drop'. He became aware of the silence and bodies lying on the sand or floating in little groups in the calm water and along the tide-line, and the rows of wrecked and abandoned vehicles and guns, like a vast ugly soundless graveyard. Groups of French soldiers of the rearguard who had fought every inch of the way back were staring out to sea, among them a few British gunners, for whom also there was now no chance of rescue.

'Who's going to bring *them* out?' he wondered. 'What about the ones left behind? What's it all for? Who's responsible?' He had seen some terrible things since the war had started but none had awed him as much as this.

In the early morning of 4 June, as the formal surrender of the town was being made by General Beaufrère, and the last survivors were appearing in England, the medical orderlies who had been left behind were being told to say 'Rotes Kreuz—nicht schiessen', 'Red Cross—don't shoot'. For the most part it worked. At the casualty clearing station at Rosendael, a German horse artillery company arrived at dawn. They were friendly and sympathetic and moved among the wounded with water, food and cigarettes. Curiously, it was a medical officer who showed the most harshness, ordering the evacuation of everybody within fifteen minutes. From then on, the wounded were treated callously until they reached Belgian hospitals where they were cared for by Belgian nursing staff. Langley was still lying on his stretcher in the casualty clearing station behind the dunes when the Germans arrived. They were quite as exhausted as the British, reeling with fatigue, coated with dust and unshaven. Two of them sank to the ground right alongside his stretcher and more a few moments later. A few days later his arm was amputated. Despite the loss, in September he escaped from the hospital he had been sent to and managed to arrive home almost a year later via Gibralter, to become involved in organising routes for Allied servicemen in occupied territory.

Reaching London, Alexander had gone to see Eden at the War Office. He was quiet and still debonair but modest about what had been done. When congratulated, he replied, 'We weren't pressed, you know'.

Nevertheless, there was a faint sense of guilt in government circles at the numbers of French who had been left behind. They had defended the perimeter for four days longer than expected, fighting for every house and every foot of ground, and there was an uneasy feeling that perhaps they had been let down. But there was also a feeling of euphoria, almost as if a victory had been won, and Churchill, who had expected to have to announce the greatest military disaster in British history, still had to make it plain that there was nothing to crow about. 'Wars,' he told the House of Commons, 'are not won by evacuations.'

Nevertheless, Dunkirk had started something. The spirit of Britain was roused, a vast flame of self-sacrifice and endeavour which swept the country and kept it going through the next dark eighteen months. In this campaign there had been no differentiation by rank. Everybody, from the commanding general downwards, had faced the same conditions, the same dangers and the same hardships. All the privileges of peacetime had disappeared and there grew from it not only inter-service co-operation but also that tremendous comradeship that carried the forces through Alamein to Normandy.

The new spirit awoke spontaneously as Churchill's blazing faith rallied the country after the deep despond of the Chamberlain Government. He made the British *want* to win the war, but he gave them no false promises, offering them only blood, toil, sweat and tears, although he made it clear also, not only to Hitler, but to the rest of the world, and most important of all, to the Americans, that the British would defend their island whatever the cost. 'We shall fight on the beaches,' he said, 'we shall fight on the landing-grounds, in the fields, in the streets and in the hills. We shall never surrender.'

The defiance did not go unnoticed. 'So long as the English tongue survives,' *The New York Times* said, 'the word Dunkirk will be spoken with reverence. In that harbour . . . at the end of a lost battle, the rags and blemishes that had hidden the soul of democracy fell away. There, beaten but unconquered, in shining splendour, she faced the enemy, this shining thing in the souls of free men which Hitler cannot command . . . It is the future. It is victory.'

It was not quite. Victory could not be made from 390,000 casualties, 68,111 of them British, or the loss of 1,000 guns and the transport, ammunition, stores and petrol for a whole army. Nevertheless, some guns, some vehicles, some ammunition and some stores and petrol were brought back and instead of the 45,000 men which were all that had been expected, 339,226 had been saved, 139,911 of them French.

The Alliance had also been saved and, what was most important, a vast group of men, battle-hardened, knowing the Germans, knowing that with the right weapons and the right leadership, they could beat the Nazi supermen. These men were available, not only to stave off invasion, but also to rebuild the armies. It was a long slog that was to go on for almost two years, but at the end of that time they swept forward with the Americans and the Russians, carrying everything before them.

Appendix:
Composition of the B.E.F. 1939–40

Commander-in-Chief: General Lord Gort, VC
C.G.S: Lt-General H. R. Pownall

GHQ TROOPS
12th Bn Royal Lancers
4/7 Bn Royal Dragoon Guards
5th Bn Inniskilling Dragoon Guards
13/18th Bn Royal Hussars
15/19th Bn King's Royal Hussars
1st Bn Fife and Forfar Yeomanry
1st Bn East Riding Yeomanry
4th and 7th Bns Royal Tank Regiment

FIRST CORPS (Lt-General M. G. H. Barker)
1ST DIVISION (Maj-General Hon. H.R.L.G. Alexander)
1st Guards Brigade
3rd Bn Grenadier Guards
2nd Bn Coldstream Guards
2nd Bn Hampshire Regiment
2nd Infantry Brigade
1st Bn North Staffordshire Regiment
6th Bn Gordon Highlanders
3rd Infantry Brigade
1st Bn Duke of Wellington's Regiment
2nd Bn Sherwood Foresters
1st Bn King's Shropshire Light Infantry
2ND DIVISION (Major-General H. C. Lloyd)
4th Infantry Brigade
1st Bn Royal Scots
2nd Bn Royal Norfolk Regiment
1/8th Bn Lancashire Fusiliers
5th Infantry Brigade

1st Bn Queen's Own Cameron Highlanders
2nd Bn Dorsetshire Regiment
7th Bn Worcestershire Regiment
6th Infantry Brigade
1st Bn Royal Welsh Fusiliers
1st Bn Royal Berkshire Regiment
2nd Bn Durham Light Infantry
48TH DIVISION (Major-General A. F. A. N. Thorne)
143rd Infantry Brigade
1st Bn Oxford & Buckinghamshire Light Infantry
5th Bn Royal Warwicks
1/7th Bn Royal Warwicks
144th Infantry Brigade
2nd Bn Royal Warwicks
5th Bn Gloucestershire Regiment
8th Bn Worcestershire Regiment
145th Infantry Brigade
2nd Bn Gloucestershire Regiment
4th Bn Oxford & Buckinghamshire Light Infantry
1st (Buckinghamshire Bn) Oxfordshire & buckinghamshire Light Infantry

SECOND CORPS (Lt-General A. F. Brooke)
3RD DIVISION (Major-General B. L. Montgomery)
7th Guards Brigade
1st Bn Grenadier Guards
2nd Bn Grenadier Guards
1st Bn Coldstream Guards
8th Infantry Brigade
1st Bn Suffolk Regiment
2nd Bn East Yorkshire Regiment
4th Bn Royal Berkshire Regiment
9th Infantry Brigade
2nd Bn Lincolnshire Regiment
1st Bn King's own Scottish Borderers
2nd Bn Royal Ulster Rifles
4TH DIVISION (Major-General D. G. Johnson)
10th Infantry Brigade
2nd Bn Bedfordshire Regiment
2nd Bn Duke of Cornwall's Light Infantry
6th Bn East Surrey Regiment

11th Infantry Brigade
2nd Bn Lancashire Fusiliers
1st Bn East Surrey Regiment
5th Bn Northamptonshire Regiment
12th Infantry Brigade
2nd Bn Royal Fusiliers
1st Bn South Lancashire Regiment
6th Bn Black Watch
50TH DIVISION (Major-General Le Q. Martel)
150th Infantry Brigade
4th Bn East Yorkshire Regi8ment
4th Bn Green Howards
5th Bn Green Howards
151st Infantry Brigade
6th Bn Durham Light Infantry
8th Bn Durham Light Infantry
9th Bn Durham Light Infantry
25th Infantry Brigade
1/7 Bn Queen's Royal Regiment
2nd Bn Essex Regiment
1st Bn Royal Irish Fusiliers

THIRD CORPS (Lt-General Sir R. F. Adam)
42ND DIVISION (Major-General W. G. Holmes)
125th Infantry Brigade
1st Bn Border Regiment
5th Bn Lancashire Fusiliers
6th Bn Lancashire Fusiliers
126th Infantry Brigade
1st Bn East Lancashire Regiment
5th Bn King's Own Royal Regiment
5th Bn Border Regiment
127th Infantry Brigade
4th Bn East Lancashire Regiment
5th Bn Manchester Regiment
1st Bn Highland Light Infantry
44TH DIVISION (Major-General E. A. Osborne)
131st Infantry Brigade
2nd Bn The Buffs
5th Bn Queen's Regiment
6th Bn Queen's Regiment

132nd Infantry Brigade
1st Bn Queen's Own Royal West Kent Regiment
4th Bn Queen's Own Royal West Kent Regiment
5th Bn Queen's Own Royal West Kent Regiment
133rd Infantry Brigade
2nd Bn Royal Sussex Regiment
4th Bn Royal Sussex Regiment
5th Bn Royal Sussex Regiment

GHQ RESERVE

5TH DIVISION (Major-General H. E. Franklyn)
13th Infantry Brigade
2nd Bn Cameronians
2nd Bn Royal Inniskilling Fusiliers
2nd Bn Wiltshire Regiment
17th Infantry Brigade
2nd Bn Royal Scots Fusiliers
2nd Bn Northamptonshire Regiment
6th Bn Seaforth Highlanders
12TH DIVISION (Major-General R. L. Petre)
35th Infantry Brigade
2/5th Bn Queen's Royal Regiment
2/6th Bn Queen's Royal Regiment
2/7th Bn Queen's Royal Regiment
36th Infantry Brigade
5th Bn The Buffs
6th Bn Queen's Own Royal West Kent Regiment
7th Bn Queen's Own Royal West Kent Regiment
37th Infantry Brigade
2/6th Bn East Surrey Regiment
6th Bn Royal Sussex Regiment
7th Bn Royal Sussex Regiment
23RD DIVISION (Major-General A. E. Herbert)
69th Infantry Brigade
5th Bn East Yorkshire Regiment
6th Bn Green Howards
7th Bn Green Howards
70th Infantry Brigade
10th Bn Durham Light Infantry
11th Bn Durham Light Infantry
1st Bn Tyneside Scottish

46TH INFANTRY DIVISION (Major-General H. C. Curtis)
137th Infantry Brigade
2/5th Bn West Yorkshire Regiment
2/6th Bn Duke of Wellington's Regiment
2/7th Bn Duke of Wellington's Regiment
38th Infantry Brigade
6th Bn Lincolnshire Regiment
2/4th Bn King's Own Yorkshire Light Infantry
6th Bn York & Lancaster Regiment
139th Infantry Brigade
2/5th Bn Leicestershire Regiment
2/5th Bn Sherwood Foresters
9th Bn Sherwood Foresters
51ST INFANTRY DIVISION (Major-General V. M. Fortune)
(Serving on Saar Front Under French Command, 10 May 1940.
Later in action south of River Somme.)
152nd Infantry Brigade
2nd Bn Seaforth Highlanders
4th Bn Seaforth Highlanders
4th Bn Queen's Own Cameron Highlanders
153rd Infantry Brigade
4th Bn Black Watch
1st Bn Gordon Highlanders
5th Bn Gordon Highlanders
154th Infantry Brigade
1st Bn Black Watch
7th Bn Argyll & Sutherland Highlanders
8th Bn Argyll & Sutherland Highlanders
1ST ARMOURED DIVISION (Major-General R. Evans)
(In action south of River Somme, except one Bn at Calais)
2nd Armoured Brigade
The Queen's Bays
9th Royal Lancers
10th Royal Hussars
3rd Armoured Brigade
2nd Bn Royal Tank Corps
3rd Bn Royal Tank Corps
3rd Bn Royal Tank Corps
5th Bn Royal Tank Corps
1st Support Group
101st L.A.A. Anti-Tank Regiment

The following two brigades also joined the BEF between mid-May and mid-June

20th Guards Brigade (to Boulogne)
2nd Bn Irish Guards
2nd Bn Welsh Guards
30th Brigade (to Calais)
2nd Bn King's Royal Rifles Corps
1st Bn Rifle Brigade
1st Bn Queen Victoria Rifles
52ND DIVISION (Major-General J. S. Drew)
155th Infantry Brigade
7/9 Bn Royal Scots
4th Bn King's Own Scottish Borderers
5th Bn King's Own Scottish Borderers
156th Infantry Brigade
4/5th Bn Royal Scots Fusiliers
6th Bn Queen's Own Cameron Highlanders
7th Bn Queen's Own Cameron Highlanders
157th Infantry Brigade
1st Bn The Glasgow Highlanders
5th Bn Highland Light Infantry
6th Bn Highland Light Infantry

Each corps and division also had its own Artillery, Engineers and other units.

Bibliography

Bartlett, Sir Basil. *My First War* (Chatto and Windus 1940)

Brickhill, Paul. *Reach For The Sky* (Collins 1957)

Collier, Richard. *The Sands of Dunkirk* (Collins 1961)

Colville, J. R. *Man of Valour* (Collins 1972)

Crisp, Robert. *Brazen Chariots* (Muller 1959)

Daniell, David S. *History of the East Surrey Regiment* (Benn 1957)

Deere, Alan. *Nine Lives* (Hodder & Stoughton 1959)

Divine, David. *Dunkirk* (Faber 1945)

Embry, Sir Basil. *Mission Completed* (Methuen 1957)

Fergusson, Bernard. *The Black Watch and The King's Enemies* (Collins 1950)

Forrester, Larry. *Fly For Your Life* (Muller 1956)

Godfrey, Major E. G. *History of the Duke of Cornwall's Light Infantry* (1966)

'Gun Buster'. *Return Via Dunkirk* (Hodder & Stoughton 1940)

Howard, Michael and Sparrow, John. *The Coldstream Guards* (Oxford University Press 1951)

Jackson, W. G. F. *Alexander of Tunis* (Batsford 1971)

Langley, J. M. *Fight Another Day* (Collins 1974)

Lewin, Ronald (Ed). *The War On Land* (Hutchinson 1969)

Martineau, G. D. *History of the Royal Sussex Regiment* (1955)

Masefield, John, *The Twenty-Five Days* (Heinemann 1972)

Mays, Spike. *No More Soldiering For Me* (Eyre and Spottiswoode 1971)

Neave, Airey. *The Flames of Calais* (Eyre and Spottiswoode 1971)

Nicolson, Nigel. *The Grenadier Guards* (Gale and Polden 1949)

Nicolson, Nigel. *Alex* (Weidenfeld and Nicolson 1973)

Richey, Paul. *Fighter Pilot* (Batsford 1941)

Spears, Major-General Sir Edward. *Assignment to Catastrophe* (Heinemann 1954)

Stewart, Captain P. F. *A History of the 12th Royal Lancers* (Oxford University Press 1950)

Thompson, Laurence. 1940 (Collins 1966)

Tute, Warren. *Escape Route Green* (Dent 1971)

Historical Records of the Queen's Own Cameron Highlanders (Blackwood 1952)